Danela Sell | Joachim Thaeter

A Pioneer
of Space Flight

Manfred Fuchs – The Biography

Carl Schünemann Verlag

"Happiness in life comes from a positive attitude"

(Manfred Fuchs in his speech at the Overeschs' silver wedding anniversary, drawing on the words of Marc Aurel)

Preface

This biography begins with an apology to its subject. The visionary space entrepreneur Manfred Fuchs was someone who loved the limelight. However, he always acknowledged those on whose shoulders he stood. They numbered a great many people over the course of his eventful life. He himself would have mentioned each one of them by name in one of his almost legendary speeches. Unfortunately, we are not able to go to such lengths in this book.

Besides, he touched the space industry in too many ways for us to give even a half-decent account of them, as his best friend Prof. Erich Overesch once remarked in his address at the conferral of Manfred Fuchs' honorary professorship. The success story of OHB itself and its technical achievements and accomplishments, which of course are inextricably linked with Manfred

Fuchs, have already been the subject of two jubilee publications. Now it's time to take a closer look at the exceptional man behind them and his career.

Originally, Christa and Marco Fuchs asked us – two former OHB employees who knew the family – to go through the professional legacy of the man who was respectfully called "Professor" by all.

Manfred Fuchs was an avid collector who wrote down his work-related ideas and plans every day, so there is a wealth of material.

As we gradually realised the depth of his impressive and multifaceted personality from the papers and personal notes, the idea of writing a book about his life and work was born. When we were at OHB, many employees paid us a visit while we worked, and all of them positively raved about their charismatic boss. We turned what started out as casual conversations into interviews to give substance to the characteristics that kept coming up and to flesh out the details of Manfred Fuchs' contribution to space flight and his success story. Unfortunately, some of his closest associates – notably Hans Hoffmann, Alfred Tegtmeier, Wolfgang Wienss and Hans Rath – are also no longer with us. However, we both knew Manfred Fuchs personally: as a boss, as a family friend and as an incredibly approachable person. With this knowledge and the information gleaned from our collection of documents, notes and images, we were able to create a complete picture of the man, his life and his life's work.

The first section of the biography is structured chronologically. It gives an account of Manfred Fuchs' life and work based on the significant milestones in his life. Then, because words such as "visionary", "entrepreneur" and "family man" came up again and again in the interviews we conducted, we devoted separate chapters to each of these characteristics and included plenty of pictures, just as Manfred Fuchs would have liked. He was a very visual person, who simply loved photos and had cabinets and shelves full of them, both in his office and at home.

Enjoy reading and leafing through the book. We hope you find it a source of inspiration, optimism and courage to explore new horizons, just as we did!

Danela Sell   Joachim Thaeter

Foreword
Prof. Ernesto Vallerani

In a world where charismatic personalities are a rarity nowadays in almost every sector, Professor Manfred Fuchs' character truly shone out in the field of international space activities.

He was a leading figure in the arena of German and European industrial enterprises for almost half a century, supporting the development of significant presences in the growing sector of space undertakings which are propelling our society towards the future.

Since I first met him in the early sixties, at a time when our two professional careers were developing in parallel along with many occasions for cooperation on various European space programmes, I remained constantly impressed by Manfred's enthusiasm and positive approach to solving the contingent problems. Over the years, our friendship not only grew closer, but also extended beyond professional occasions to the extent that our families would meet together privately, which gave us the opportunity to get to know one another better and better.

The more I got to know him, the more complex his personality seemed to me. First and foremost, he was an engineer, but he was never very keen on technical details and scientific disquisitions. He knew what he was talking about, he understood the problems and the difficulties of a given endeavour, but he was also fascinated by the opportunities and by the challenges of realising an undertaking often anything but simple.

Manfred possessed an innate "business sense", which drove him to identify opportunities and discover ways of utilising them, but he was by no means merely an opportunist attracted solely by the benefits he expected to reap; he evaluated each and every business opportunity not only from a profit perspective, but also with an aim to finding in it an occasion to venture into an enterprise that would test his skills. He was not afraid of risks. In some ways, he relished them, as it was a chance to prove to himself that he was able to overcome the difficulties.

In a contest in which, in more recent years especially, the leaders responsible for the major space industries have tended to be more and more financial and business people rather than space personalities, Manfred represented a somewhat isolated example of a visionary space entrepreneur, attentive to new concepts, attracted by new ideas, open to innovation – a man always looking far ahead of the times, towards the future.

Professor Manfred Fuchs will be remembered by the international space community for his many achievements during his long and successful career, beginning with the time when he was employed at ERNO Space Technology GmbH in Bremen, with leading responsibilities in several European programmes such as Ariane, Spacelab and several application and scientific satellites of the M.E.S.H consortium. He played a fundamental role in the inception of the Columbus programme, conceived by an Aeritalia Space System Group initiative and promoted initially as an Italo-German programme before evolving into the European Space Agency's (ESA) largest contribution to the International Space Station (ISS).

However, Manfred's personality could not be restrained by a large, bureaucratic, industrial organisation; his spirit of independence, probably rooted in his South Tyrolean origins, led him to attempt the venture of establishing his own space company after his own style.

It was the founding of OHB together with his talented wife, Christa, at the beginning of the eighties which gave Manfred the long-sought-after opportunity to realise his immense potential of "boss, businessman, spaceman" to its fullest extent.

And it truly was an extraordinary international success, an exacting heritage that he left all too soon in the capable hands of his son, Marco, who is committed to continuing the dream of a visionary that has become a concrete reality.

Thank you, Manfred, for all you did for all of us involved in supporting Europe's contribution to the expansion of Human presence beyond Earth's terrestrial boundaries.

E. Vallerani

Per Aspera ad Astra.
Prof. E. Vallerani

"Poggio Cusiano", Miasino, June 2017

Foreword
Prof. Heinz Stoewer

Manfred Fuchs was an exceptional leadership personality:

- As an engineer a visionary, someone with great intuition for the right solution

- As an industrial leader a decision maker, who knew which course to charter and which risks to accept

- As a leader of people a motivator, someone who could inspire and get his teams to go to great lengths in winning or executing projects

These qualities were at the source of his unprecedented success! Whenever we assessed a complex project, if needs be over a good glass of wine, in the end he would come up with the "intuition" for the right technical solution or the cleverest business opportunity. And he was an innovator – always searching for the better, simpler, cheaper idea. It was amazing to work with him. He could listen most attentively, reason and argue, but eventually he took the right decisions, no matter how risky!

Manfred could create deep personal bonds with partners anywhere in the aerospace community, be it in Germany, Europe or anywhere else. We started working together already in the 1960s on the first European launcher, he in Bremen, me in Ottobrunn, both very young. These were "start-up" times for German and European space, a period which marked both of us strongly along the lines: "everything is possible" or "the sky is the limit". Manfred never lost this attitude. It was one of his strong personality trademarks.

He was respected and trusted because of his integrity, transparency and honesty. While at times he would fight his competitors to crucial "win or lose" battles, he could also be generous in making deals with them, which in the end mostly resulted in a win-win for all, be it in Bremen, Munich, Friedrichshafen or anywhere else in Europe. Competing **and** cooperating was his motto. And he always reminded everyone to remain fair, since he knew that in our small space world, a competitor of today could be a most valuable and needed partner of tomorrow.

Manfred was one of the inventors of the Columbus idea as the European participation in the ISS. Together with Ernesto Vallerani from Aeritalia and Gottfried Greger from the German Research and Technology Ministry he fought to convince politicians, scientists and anyone else prepared to listen to get this idea realized. It was to a good extent "his baby", one that he remained proud of even though OHB in the end only had a small part in its final development. He was happy that the German and European lead was secured for Bremen, his professional hometown.

Family was a most important treasure to him. Notably Christa, Romana and Marco along with the extended South Tyrolean family were always in his focus and at his heart. Most remarkable was how he took to the idea to withdraw little by little as Marco in turn took over more and more of the OHB Group's leadership functions. He knew he could rely on the qualities and exceptional education of Marco to continue the OHB success. Manfred's wisdom enabled an almost unheard of smooth governance transition at the top of this family

enterprise. He could "let go" and in turn spend more time on some of his favourite topics, e.g. the Moon and the Max Valier microsatellite, built in part by students from his former technical college in Bolzano.

His sudden death sent reverberations through the entire aerospace community in industry, politics and academia as well as his long-term professional friends. A wave of expressions of deep respect and genuine sympathy unparalleled in our aerospace world followed. We miss him in many situations, but feel inspired for being able to continue along the path he had set out.

Prof. Dipl.-Ing. Heinz Stoewer, M. Sc.
Long-time professional friend and associate

Foreword
Bernd Neumann

I first met Manfred Fuchs in the 1970s and our paths took the same course for a long time. I got to know and value him both professionally and privately during this period.

I can recall more than a few inaugurations to which he invited me to speak in an official capacity, which documented the steady growth of his firm. When OHB was still a young company, I was Deputy Minister under Heinz Riesenhuber at the Ministry of Research in Bonn. We often worked together, as the space industry also came under the remit of my Ministry. Over time, the projects we worked on together gave rise to very close, cordial ties, that I remember fondly and am glad to have been a part of.

At that stage, we already knew each other from the Bremen arm of the CDU. From the outset, Manfred Fuchs was very involved in the party and was a deputy in the CDU citizens' group. He was curious, innovative and always wanted to effect change. Later, after 1990, he began to compile the first space programme for the CDU together with other experts, first at federal state level and later also for the party in Bonn. In doing so, he saw himself as a visionary, looking far into the future. Manfred Fuchs tried by every means available to him to pitch space flight to each and everyone involved, especially those in politics. He was the one who reiterated to me time and time again during my Deputy Minister days why it was so important for us to be involved in the ISS. He was a terrific networker, both in politics and in the various fields of research, and ultimately this explains his professional success. It explains how on more than one occasion he obtained the approval that was needed to fund new space projects. In latter times, I recall conversations where he was adamant that flight to Mars should be the next mission. In his space endeavours, he convinced many politicians of his goals and visions: for example, Franz Josef Strauss in the 1980s.

German Chancellor Angela Merkel expressly thanked him again for his commitment in 2013.

However, Manfred Fuchs was interested in other things besides space and politics. He had many facets to his personality. He was also a major and frequent patron of the arts, which I was particularly pleased about later, of course, in my role as Minister for Culture and Media. For example, he supported the Bremen classical music festival and endowed a professorship at the university. On the supervisory board of the German Aerospace Center (DLR) – when I was Chairman and he was my deputy – we both fought for and succeeded in enforcing greater consideration for the SME sector in the awarding of space contracts than in the past.

Our work relationship developed into a friendship and our families also got to know each other better. We had good times together in his home town of Latsch. I have fond memories of Christmas holidays in particular. It was in Latsch that I got to know his whole family, who were so very important to him. One could tell how highly regarded he was in his home town, where he was dubbed "the satellite guy"! Manfred Fuchs was a very generous friend. His was an enduring friendship that he maintained and cultivated.

Bernd Neumann

Two spacemen of the first hour: astronaut Buzz Aldrin, second person on the Moon in 1969, and Manfred Fuchs, who played a central role in building up the space industry in Germany and Europe.

Contents

1938–
1959

"Medl Fuchs' young lad"

Manfred's father Romedius, known as Medl, (*30th August 1909 † 6th April 1988) was a tall, handsome and kindly man who ran a small transport business in Latsch.

Manfred Johannes Fuchs came into the world in the small market town of Latsch in the Vinschgau Valley in South Tyrol on 25th July 1938. Self-reliance and entrepreneurship ran in his family going back to the 13th century. His parents were haulier Romedius (nicknamed Medl) and Paula, née Laimer. Manfred's grandfather was local legend, sawmill operator Josef Fuchs, the first Vinschgau native to own a truck. Josef's three-storey house by the sawmill was also home to his children and their families, including Manfred's parents, Manfred and siblings Romed – just one year younger than Manfred – and Ingeburga, who was born in 1941. Romedius was an aviation fanatic and named his first-born son after Manfred von Richthofen, the flying ace from World War I. Perhaps that was where Manfred Fuchs' passion for aviation stemmed from, perhaps not, but in any case, flying would play a big role in his life and work. The young boy grew up against the backdrop of World War II. Contemporaries say that Latsch saw little of the war. Fighter planes, which frightened residents, passed over and every so often soldiers passed through the village on their way to Bolzano, but otherwise the market town was "strategically unimportant". Most of the men were off at war. Fortunately, father Romedius returned unscathed from action in Italy quite soon, as Romed related.

Meanwhile, Manfred, who was growing up to be tall and slim, went to nursery in Latsch and struck up what would turn out to be a lifelong friendship with Josef "Sepp" Rinner. Together the two fine young lads started primary school in Latsch on 5th September 1944 and shared a bench in Mr Federspiel's class. Manfred was described as a rather average pupil overall, but good at mathematics and arithmetic. He got on well with the children who interested him, the others "he ignored completely," said fellow pupils Dorothea "Thea" Mitterer and Aloisia "Luise" Stricker. The same went for activities at break-time. If Manfred had no interest in doing something, he didn't bother; "he always had a stubborn streak."

In 1947, Romedius and Paula built their own house at Marktstrasse 27, opposite the playing field "Am Moos". This was where the children from the upper part of Latsch congregated. Manfred, too, and his siblings and

25th July 1938

Manfred Johannes Fuchs is born in Latsch, South Tyrol

5th September 1944

Starts primary school in Latsch along with his friend Josef "Sepp" Rinner

Mother Paula with her
children Romed, Inge and
Manfred (right)

friends spent a lot of time there, but no one who hung around with him at the time would describe him as being particularly sporty. Apart from a bit of football and a brief stint of discus-throwing in the school championships, his obsession with technology occupied most of his time even then. Manfred cut pictures of planes out of magazines and stuck them into scrapbooks or made model aeroplanes out of cardboard.

"The Fuchses know their machines, but not their Bible"

There are tales of Manfred, still at primary-school age, searching here, there and everywhere for parts to build a radio, which he put into operation in the school store. No wonder the minister at the time coined the phrase, much repeated to this very day, "The Fuchses know their machines, but not their Bible". The children did go to church, "because it was the done thing," but they sometimes gave it a miss and they didn't excel at Bible studies.

South Tyrol was a poor region at that time. "Almost everyone was a farmer. In principle, we were all self-sufficient. There was enough to eat, but there was no money. Despite that, we did all right," recalled Romed. While his father, a 6'2" tall, sincere,

Young Manfred in front of his mother's bar. Here he often played cards and sometimes won up to 20 espressos in a day.

hard-working and unpretentious man, spent the whole day delivering for the most part construction materials for family homes in his truck, Paula obtained the licence to set up the regional branch of the ENAL (Ente nazionale assistenza lavoratori) national workers assistance organisation on the ground floor of their new home. At that time, the organisation had around 2.5 million members across over 13,600 clubs and subsidised leisure time activities for labourers. Paula Fuchs' ENAL branch was a small Pools agent with three tables and a bar. The establishment soon blossomed into the local place to go for gossip and playing cards. In the midst of the comings and goings was Manfred, who learned a lot here for later life. For example, while he would later love socialising and did so often, he hardly ever drank alcohol to excess, probably because he saw the downside more than once for himself. His mother Paula was a born hostess, playing cards with her patrons until the wee hours, sometimes for high stakes. She stood out from the country folk with her statuesque, well-groomed appearance. She came from Lana near Meran and had trained as a housekeeper with a count near Padua. As a result, she spoke good Italian, which she taught her children. This would also turn out to be highly beneficial to Manfred in the course of his life. Paula is also described as being gracious, resolute, dominant, sociable and active. She was involved in the theatrical society as a prompter and costume designer. The children grew up in what was a

very unusual environment for the time and the conservative Catholic society, where their "mother ruled the roost" and all ethnic groups were tolerated.

While Paula was reputed to be quite strict, Romedius was by all accounts a kindly man. He often put benches in the bed of his truck to drive his children's classes to church in Riffian near Meran. Romedius and Paula, though money was tight, always supported Manfred's dreams of becoming an engineer. After he finished seventh grade they allowed the teenager to leave the school in Latsch and begin his mechanical engineering schooling at Bolzano technical college. He and his friend Sepp Rinner moved to Bolzano, around 60 kilometres away, and became independent at the young age of just 13. The two shared a room in Draxl guesthouse and they attended school together for another four years before their interests drifted apart towards the end of their school education. While Sepp opted for building construction in his final year, Manfred stuck with engineering and finished his studies on 21st June 1956 to become a qualified mechanical engineer. That school, too, (today the Max Valier College of Technology) would later play an important role in his life once again.

While at college in Bolzano, his visits home were confined to weekends and holidays, when Manfred, like the years before, nailed together fruit crates in the Fuchs' sawmill to earn a little pocket money. Then, at 16,

August 1951

At the age of 13 Manfred switches to Bolzano technical college to begin his specialised education

he had a stroke of luck when he heard about a competition organised by the Aero Club d'Italia for flight training, which he went on to win. Just one year later, on 12th July 1956, he obtained his licence from the Aviazione Civile Italiana, making him Italy's youngest pilot at the age of 17. His achievement fuelled his desire to become either a pilot with his own airline or even a fighter pilot. Manfred himself said he tried in vain to convince his father to include aeroplanes in the family's transport services. His mother Paula feared for Manfred's life and was not particularly enthusiastic about either possible outcome. She persuaded her son to get a proper education first. A teacher in Bolzano told Manfred about the good opportunities to study engineering in Germany. And so, in 1956, the young man moved to Munich for the winter semester, again with the financial support of his family, to study mechanical engineering at the Higher Technical Education Institute. His sister Inge followed him to earn money as a maid. The two of them lived in the Ramersdorf district with the Bernardi family of engineers, whom they knew from Latsch. Manfred often walked the almost nine kilometres from his accommodation to the Technical Institute. Money was tight, and his parents had to scrimp and save. The young student did everything in his power to do his bit by being thrifty. After just one year in Munich, in September 1957, the ambitious student transferred to engineering school in Hamburg and registered for the Automotive and

Flying was Manfred's passion from an early age. He took flying lessons for his pilot's licence at the airfield in Bolzano. He had his picture taken with his friend Sepp (on the left) standing in front of a Noratlas at St. Jakob airfield.

21st June 1956

Graduates from Bolzano technical college

12th July 1956

At 17, Manfred receives his pilot's licence, making him the youngest pilot in Italy

The 12 m free fall jump in Bolzano in 1956 doubled as a test of courage and a parachute jump test for Manfred's pilot's licence.

Aeronautical Engineering course. The facilities there better suited his interests, as the faculty had been using the wind tunnel left behind by shipbuilders since 1956. The wind tunnel meant that the subjects aerodynamics and flight mechanics could be added to the programme of study, and these were the examination subjects which Manfred Fuchs subsequently chose.

In Hamburg, he started off subletting in the St. Georg district right beside the school. The third semester had already begun when Manfred Fuchs, dressed in a brown leather jacket and red jumper, entered the full classroom and lecturer Dr Volkersen directed him to the front row. Grudgingly, all the students moved up to make room for the youngest in the class. Their resentment didn't last long, as Manfred Fuchs soon made friends thanks to his "fun, enthusiastic, moderate, respectful, genuine and determined nature". In particular, he immediately made friends with the boy sitting to his left, Enrique Ortiz; a friendship that would last long after they left university. The two of them as well as Amin Stephan and Sebastian Buskell formed an inseparable clique who discussed the lectures in-depth and spent their free time together. They regularly ate lunch near Hamburg Central Train Station in a place that served meals for less than two Deutschmarks. They ran the risk of an upset stomach but, as all four were hard up, they didn't have much choice despite the range on offer in Hamburg. That didn't stop them from

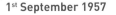

1st September 1957

Manfred transfers from the Technical Institute in Munich to engineering school in Hamburg

4th October 1957

Sputnik is the first satellite in space

having fun and enjoying themselves, though, as the fellow students recall happily. In particular, they have vivid memories of a ten-day study trip around West Germany, aimed at giving the future engineers an overview of their career prospects. They talk of missed youth hostel curfews and having to break in, and of drinking wine and singing along to an accordion on the bus. And as socialising ran in his blood, Manfred Fuchs was always one of the ringleaders. So, naturally, he was at a Carnival party in Cap Polonio Hotel in Pinneberg in February 1959, where he had an encounter that would have far-reaching consequences for the young South Tyrolean: he met a young, pretty, blonde woman. The only two unmasked partygoers were standing in the gallery of the premises watching the goings-on below them. Manfred spoke to her, and there was an immediate spark. Her name was Christa Köper. Both abandoned their incensed dates at the party and were inseparable from that evening on.

In the meantime, Manfred had moved to the more affordable town of Rellingen near Pinneberg, so the two now often took the train into the centre of Hamburg: he to school and she to her commercial apprenticeship at the Klöckner steel company. At that time, Manfred was in the middle of writing his thesis: a design for an 8-seater passenger aircraft. He finished his studies on 30th September 1959 after completing his sixth semester. The door to the future was now wide open to the young engineer, a future involving the rebuilding of the Federal Republic of Germany. Even before being awarded his degree certificate, he began working in design for the aircraft manufacturer Hamburger Flugzeugbau (HFB) on 1st October 1959. At that time, HFB employed around 300 people. He also joined the German Aero Club (DAeC) and continued to fly in his spare time.

Together with his fellow students from the engineering school in Hamburg, Manfred went on a study trip around West Germany.

February 1959

Christa and Manfred meet at a Carnival party in Pinneberg

Christa and Manfred Fuchs were inseparable from when they met in February
1959 and that same year they travelled to
Latsch, where these pictures were taken.

1ˢᵗ October 1959

Manfred starts work as a designer
at Hamburger Flugzeugbau

1960–
1984

The sky's the limit

On 1st February 1960, Manfred Fuchs received his official certificate of qualification. This bestowed upon the ambitious young man the title of aeronautical and automotive engineer at the tender age of 21, and he was made permanent in the Aerodynamics/Flight Mechanics department by HFB. His career started on the new projects "Commercial Aircraft HFB 115F/320" and "Transall C160".

Privately, having introduced his girlfriend Christa to the family in Latsch in August 1959, Manfred began looking for somewhere for them to live together because they were expecting their first child. He found what he was looking for in a villa in Hamburg-Othmarschen. The young, as yet unmarried, couple moved into the spacious living quarters on the upper floor at the beginning of 1960. His choice made it instantly clear that Manfred was "drawn to prestige, to fine things and to castles" as his daughter Romana later put it. He could have chosen a simple apartment to start with, but Manfred decided on the villa and had no problems securing it either. Despite there being a number of candidates, the landlord, who also lived in the house, chose the man from South Tyrol because he came across as extremely charming and polite and was working as an engineer.

On 29th April 1960, Manfred and Christa were married in a civil ceremony in Pinneberg. That very same day,

the newly-weds travelled to South Tyrol to celebrate the occasion properly with the extended Fuchs family and friends. Only Manfred's mother Paula was not thrilled at that point because she had had other plans for her first-born. She had wanted him to marry the daughter of a local winemaker, return home and take over the vineyard. But Manfred would not have been Manfred if he hadn't asserted himself with charm in this important matter of life. Despite the strong ties to his homeplace and his family, there was no going back. In the agricultural region of South Tyrol it would have been difficult to pursue an engineering career, whilst in Germany the opportunities for young engineers were outstanding. Now that his heart was in the far North of Germany, all his mother's hopes for her son to return

1st February 1960

Manfred receives his certificate of qualification as an aeronautical and automotive engineer

29th April 1960

Civil wedding of Christa and Manfred in Pinneberg

were dashed. But by the time her first grandchild, a girl named Romana Manuela, was born on 12th October 1960, Paula had come to terms with her son's chosen path in life. Besides, in Christa she found an ally to talk him out of the idea of becoming a fighter pilot. It can't have been too hard to persuade him because Manfred Fuchs had always been a responsible family man. His priority was now to look after his young family, avoid unnecessarily putting himself in harm's way and kick-start his career.

In the latter respect, he was greatly helped by the establishment of the northern development consortium (Entwicklungsring Nord – ERNO) in Bremen in 1961

comprising Weser-Flugzeugbau, Focke-Wulf and his firm Hamburger Flugzeugbau. Manfred Fuchs volunteered to transfer to ERNO and made the daily commute between the two Hanseatic cities by train.

It surprised his work colleague and friend Dr Peter Natenbruck to know that he worked as a ticket inspector on the journeys to save himself the price of a ticket. "This showed how utterly pragmatic he was."

In Bremen he worked under the aeronautical pioneer Prof. Dr Gerhard Eggers initially for a period of nine months as an aeronautical engineer developing the aerodynamics of vertical and short take-off aircraft.

Manfred Fuchs moved to Entwicklungsring Nord (ERNO) as man of the first hour. He and his colleagues aimed to advance the space effort in Germany.

 12th October 1960

Birth of daughter Romana
Manuela Fuchs

 1st January 1961

Establishment of Entwicklungsring Nord
(ERNO) comprising Weser-Flugzeugbau,
Focke-Wulf and Hamburger Flugzeugbau

The test launches of the Europa rocket in Woomera, Australia, were not a resounding success but they did pave the way for the later ARIANE.

It was during this time that an important decision was made by Konrad Adenauer's cabinet that was to have lasting consequences for Manfred Fuchs: West Germany decided to collaborate with France and the UK on the development of a European launch vehicle. This marked Germany's entry into the space arena.

Prof. Eggers thought it a promising endeavour and at the beginning of 1962 he proposed to set up a space group within ERNO. The core members of the team at that time were the three intrepid young engineers Hans E. W. Hoffmann, Winfried Ruhe and Horst Billig, who have gone down in history as "the three Gagarins" for their pioneering roles in Bremen's contribution to space flight. These three would also later be friends, colleagues and trusted advisers of Manfred Fuchs. Fuchs himself was another man of the first hour, moving over to ERNO-R on 24th March 1962 and working on designs for the third stage of the Europa rocket.

Renowned rocket specialist Hans Schneider was brought on board on 1st April 1962 to head up the space group in Bremen. The team in Bremen consisted of only around twelve members. One of them was Erich Overesch, whom Manfred Fuchs would soon call his best friend. The two young men sat across from each other in the office. The later Professor of Space Technology and Catholic deacon and Manfred engaged in deep conversations about the critical questions of the universe and existence. "Where do we come from? Where are we going?" were two questions that Fuchs liked to talk about and would also raise in speeches later in life. Not only did space flight interest him from a technical point of view, but the vast expanse of space was also a philosophical wellspring for him. Manfred Fuchs thought it absurd to claim that we were alone in

12th April 1961

April 1961

Yuri Gagarin is the first man in space

Manfred transfers to ERNO in Bremen as HFB's representative

the universe, especially as more and more discoveries were being made about the extent of space and the countless galaxies it contained. For this reason, he increasingly turned his attention then and later to the scientific side of space flight and the exploration of outer space.

The atmosphere at ERNO was imaginative and inspiring. The colleagues were mutually supportive and enthusiastic about their challenging job of effectively building space expertise in Germany from the ground up. There was no question of Manfred Fuchs' returning to aeronautical engineering in Hamburg. Besides, on 29th June 1962, Christa and Manfred's second child, a boy whom they named Marco Romed, was born. Manfred decided to relocate to Bremen and bought a terraced house in the Huchting area of Bremen. The

family moved in on 18th July 1964 without having set eyes on the house beforehand. "That was typical Manfred. He organised everything, did the choosing, made the plans, then picked us up," said Christa, who arrived at the same time as the removal van.

Manfred told her it was only a stop-gap until they found a detached home that fit the bill. He didn't like the narrow build of the terraced houses. He refused to erect a fence between the plots. For one, this reflected his open personality and, for another, it encouraged a good relationship with the neighbours. As was common at

that time, many wild parties were thrown in the converted basement bars. Manfred Fuchs always invited his colleagues and superiors. He did not treat anyone differently, no matter their position in the hierarchy, and that was something all his acquaintances noticed

A meeting of the Spacelab utilisation working group takes the opportunity to visit the Spacelab model at ERNO.

14th June 1962

Establishment of the
European Space
Research Organisation
(ESRO)

29th June 1962

Birth of son Marco Romed Fuchs

Manfred loved to socialise. This photo shows him dancing with his sister-in-law Sylvia, Christa's half-sister and wife of his friend and employee Alfred Tegtmeier.

about him. Including Hans Schneider's son Gerhard, who was doing work experience at ERNO in 1964 when he met Manfred for the first time. "One could always have a good chat with him, even though he was the boss. This was when I was a lowly student and he was head of astrodynamics," said Schneider, who, after his career at ERNO, became Aerospace Coordinator for the State of Bremen and a good friend of Manfred Fuchs. With natural flair and strategic purpose he networked with people from all walks of life and all social echelons, which not only won him a lot of sympathy in the course of his life but also furthered his career.

In June 1962 his career got another boost when the two forerunners of the European Space Agency (ESA) – ESRO and ELDO – were established. For ERNO this meant publicly funded contracts, including for the development of sounding rockets, shuttles, satellites and probes. Manfred initially worked mainly on the third stage of the Europa rocket. The development team in the early years was made up of many young engineers from all the participating European countries. This was how he came to meet another important person in his life in 1964: Ernesto Vallerani from the Italian FIAT Avio team (later Aeritalia and Alenia), who would play a key role in particular during the upcoming Spacelab and Columbus phases. The two first encountered each other when Vallerani was dispatched to Bremen for a meeting. Manfred broke the ice by greeting the young man in Italian. A close friendship developed. "Manfred had a unique blend of German reliability and organisational skills combined with the dynamism and imagination of an Italian," said the later Chairman of Alenia Spazio, who also described Fuchs as a leader with very strong views. "If you agreed with him, great. If you didn't, you were in for it!" 'It' being a tirade of loud and sometimes hot-tempered shouting. But fits of temper were rare, as Manfred Fuchs had a natural authority and intrinsic self-confidence. He absolutely accepted different opinions and views but they had to be based on a fundamental willingness to cooperate and find a solution.

18th July 1964

The Fuchs family moves
to Bremen

What Vallerani and Fuchs had in common was mutual trust and the aforementioned interest in working together to the satisfaction of all sides involved in order to advance space travel in Europe. While Ernesto Vallerani was successfully building his career in Italy, in Germany, Manfred Fuchs was promoted to head of the "Systems and Mission Analysis" Predevelopment department on 1st January 1965. When ERNO, which by that time had 670 employees, became a fully fledged company in 1967, he was promoted again, this time to head of the "Aerodynamics/Flight Mechanics and Launcher System" department. In 1968, Manfred Fuchs was one of the delegation which flew out to test launch the Europa rocket in Woomera, Australia. He logged the journey, including stopovers in Karachi, Hong Kong, Manila, Papeete and Bermuda, in his private diary under the heading "Round-the-world trip". It reveals his fascination with the different sights, cultures and ways of life. He observed them closely, sought out contact with natives and put down his thoughts on paper. These were two of Manfred Fuchs' distinguishing characteristics. All his life he engaged openly with people and observed what was going on around him very closely.

While at the end of the 1960s the space endeavour in Europe and at ERNO in particular was advancing with the launches of the first scientific satellites "HEOS-1" and "Azur", the development of the Europa rocket was

"Manfred had a unique blend of German reliability and organisational skills combined with the dynamism and imagination of an Italian"

Portrait of Manfred Fuchs with his trademark broad smile.

in crisis after a number of failed launches. Manfred Fuchs and his department redoubled their efforts to enhance and improve the launcher system, applying new drive concepts. The Viking engine came about as a result of close collaboration with the French. Based on the Viking engine, France submitted its L3S launch system design (L3S was the French acronym for third-generation substitution launcher) to the ESA Ministerial Council in Brussels in 1973, which, under the name of ARIANE, would soon bring about success for an independent, European launcher system.

However, Manfred Fuchs never put all his eggs in one basket, and he and his department did the groundwork on a number of space-related issues. Aerodynamics was one of his pet projects. From 1966, he systemati-

1st January 1965

Manfred is made head of the "Systems and Mission Analysis" group at ERNO

1st July 1967

Promotion to head of the department "Aerodynamics/ Flight Mechanics and Launcher System"

32

Model of the "Bumerang" lifting body, created by ERNO in preparation for the development of a shuttle for re-entry into the Earth's atmosphere.

cally built up this section and pressed ahead with the lifting body programmes "Bumerang" and "Orbiter" on behalf of the ESA. The United States' successful moon landing on 20th/ 21st July 1969 spurred on development work on these shuttles for re-entry into the Earth's atmosphere. In the post-Apollo era, the US decided to develop the Space Shuttle and – some time later – the manned space station. Thanks to Manfred Fuchs' department's experience in development and flight,

ERNO was on board with the endeavour. However, when NASA was awarded the contract in January 1972, the US Department of Defense took over the majority of the development costs, which left Europe without a role. Fuchs did not give up, and he and his colleagues tried to find other ways and means.

"They simply wondered what sort of a payload the huge Shuttle could be used for once it was finished, because no-one else had thought about utilisation," recalled Hans Hoffmann in an interview with the Deutsches Museum in Munich. With plans for ERNO's involvement in the Shuttle's development in tatters, Fuchs pulled his utilisation programme out of the bag. "It was brilliant. Spacelab was born," said Hoffmann. Led by the ESA, Spacelab was presented in Huntsville, Alabama, on 10th December 1970, officially as a potential experimental vehicle for microgravity research, and accepted by the Americans. "Europe had secured a part in the post-Apollo programme, the US had a main payload for the Shuttle and Bremen became the centre of manned space flight in Europe," said Hoffmann.

On 1st June 1972, the Spacelab Phase A tender left ERNO. Spearheaded by ERNO, the tender had been prepared by M.E.S.H., a consortium of European aerospace companies Matra, ERNO, Saab and Hawker Siddeley that had been engineered by the ESA. M.E.S.H.'s competitors were the STAR and COSMOS consortia.

29th November 1968

Launch of Europa 1 in Woomera, Australia

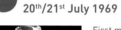

20th/21st July 1969

First manned landing on the moon

This was how the competitive structures within the European space industry came about and were consolidated. The M.E.S.H. tender ultimately won out over all the other European contenders because Manfred Fuchs' department, namely Alfred Tegtmeier and Jochen Herzog, proposed a modular structure with the flexibility to be expanded or reduced, as necessary.

Alfred Tegtmeier was a central figure in the conception of Spacelab.

From then on, manned space flight in the broader sense and research in zero gravity were Manfred Fuchs' constant occupation and areas in which he was a great influencer and promoter. Even at that point he was thinking ahead. He was dynamic. He tabled topics, lobbied for them at all levels and as soon as they were on the road to success he and his team turned their thoughts to the next move. "Manfred was not a fundamental engineer who was into the minutiae. He was more interested in developing ideas, initiating projects and then making them top of the list of priorities of all those involved. He believed it was Europe's duty to make a significant contribution to the space endeavour," recalled Vallerani. To this end, Manfred Fuchs established ASN, the Spacelab utilisation programme working group, on 23rd June 1973. ERNO, MBB and Dornier, working in the ASN with many scientists, developed the first experiments in zero-gravity research. "Manfred Fuchs used his good contacts with university institutes and other scientific institutions," said Hoffmann. He also sought support from politicians, which he received from Prof. Dr Gottfried Greger at the Ministry of Research in Bonn. From the Spacelab era on, the head of the Space division at the Ministry of Research was a close confidant, friend and supporter of Manfred Fuchs. The pair had a constructive and open working relationship because they both cared about advancing space flight with Germany's involvement. It was clear to Fuchs from early on that the cost of manned space flight could only be justified to the man on the street if it were used and the results of its missions were for the benefit of mankind. He defined the programme and supplied the arguments to be presented to the public for the budgets to receive political

Hans E. W. Hoffmann was one of the "three Gagarins" at ERNO and a long-time colleague, comrade and friend of Manfred Fuchs.

10th December 1970

Spacelab is pitched in Huntsville as a potential experiment platform for the Space Shuttle and accepted

23rd June 1973

Manfred sets up the Spacelab utilisation working group (ASN)

Manfred Fuchs and head of the Space division at the Ministry of Research Prof. Dr Gottfried Greger cared deeply about advancing the space endeavour with Germany's involvement.

approval. "The Ministry with Prof. Greger was a power-house. He was, in my view, the go-to man. He was an excellent head of division, the best I knew in my life-time. He was innovative; he believed people and acted on it," said Fuchs about his ally in an interview with the Deutsches Museum.

On 6th June 1974, ERNO was awarded the contract to develop and build Spacelab as the lead contractor within the M.E.S.H. group. "It was monumental for the European space effort," recalled Vallerani. It was a success attributable in no small way to Manfred Fuchs' commitment and signalled Europe's entry into manned space flight. This whole area, especially research in zero gravity, was greatly influenced by Fuchs and he would continue to pursue it all his life. It would include future Spacelab utilisation, the Columbus module for the International Space Station and the utilisation of smaller launch systems and drop capsules providing tolerable times to validate experiments in zero gravity. The subject of a drop tower first appeared in his records as early as 1975. The idea was conceived for the scientific utilisation programme and for cost-ef-fectively trialling the Spacelab experiments. Manfred Fuchs' proposed location was, of course, Bremen. He began lobbying politicians and started searching for interested parties.

On 1st June 1974, Manfred Fuchs was promoted to sen-ior head of the "Proposals and Studies" department. The 40-strong department would have done anything for him, as Gerhard Schneider reported, "One could talk to him about anything. He was approachable, per-suasive and unremittingly optimistic about everything and everyone. He never criticised people. Instead, he explained to them in a positive manner how something

1st June 1974

Manfred is promoted to sen-ior head of the "Proposals and Studies" department

6th June 1974

ERNO (M.E.S.H. consortium) is awarded the contract to develop Spacelab

The Spacelab model at ERNO; illustrated inside the Space Shuttle. The photo on the bottom right shows a test run on the Space Sled.

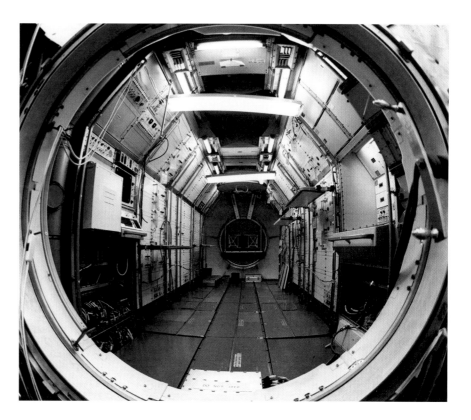

should be done better or differently. He was the perfect boss." His indulgent Christmas party speeches, in which he mentioned each and every employee by first and last name and listed their positive achievements and merits, were a feature even back in the ERNO days. What Manfred Fuchs' speeches lacked in pithiness and structure, they made up for in charm and charisma.

His duties as senior head of department now included the preparatory definitions and designs for all major space projects from launch vehicles through microgravity research to satellites and probes. In addition, he was already doing work in other areas such as marine and environmental technology. In general, what stands out from this stage of his career is that he built up a broad range of engineering capabilities in his department, including new concepts for future space missions; for example, launch vehicles, drives and test benches, mini-shuttles and low-cost experiments, re-entry, Molniya orbit, FreeFlyer, the Space Tug, X-ray satellites, space components such as the Space Sled, manipulators, experiments, heat pipes, tanks as well as terrestrial solar power plants and wind turbines, and the RESUS submarine rescue system. Manfred Fuchs structured his department to have a very broad base, giving it the flexibility to react to events and political decisions.

30th May 1975

Establishment of the
European Space Agency (ESA)

Then Canadian ambassador Donald Sutherland McPhail being presented with a model of the Spacelab by Manfred Fuchs during a visit to ERNO.

Fuchs' election as Chairman of the ASN in West Germany on 30th September 1976 meant he now sat side by side with the experts and scientists involved in microgravity research and devised pioneering utilisation programmes for Spacelab. In 1976, he was appointed to the M.E.S.H. Policy Committee, the highest body in the M.E.S.H. consortium, and in meetings again sat at the table with his friend Ernesto Vallerani. This committee was instrumental in paving the way for the European contribution to the International Space Station, the Columbus module. Manfred Fuchs even gave it its name. The original launch date was 1992, the 500th anniversary of the discovery of America by Christopher Columbus. Fuchs had always had a strong affinity for memorable, fitting project names which would make good PR and with which everyone could identify. Stoewer said in relation to this, "Manfred Fuchs always thought in European and international terms, especially European, of course. His collaboration with Vallerani was not only so very close because of where he came from, but because he knew that manned space flight in Europe was dead in the water without Italy!"

In 1977, Manfred Fuchs' Predevelopment department continued to push forward new concepts for optimising satellite construction (central tube, CFK type) in preparation for numerous upcoming national and European satellite projects. When the M.E.S.H. consortium elected him Chairman on 25th June 1978, the Eutelsat communications satellite, the MARECS maritime communications satellite and the astrometry satellite Hipparcos projects were executed with ERNO's involvement. Hipparcos was a scientific mission that was actually in the domain of ERNO's southern German competitor, who also made vigorous attempts to get in on the project. Unsuccessfully, thanks to Manfred Fuchs' personal efforts.

The first successful launch of the ARIANE rocket took place on 24th December 1979. ERNO, as before, was responsible for the third stage. As the launch vehicle became more successful, the project gained increasing independence in organisational terms and moved off Manfred Fuchs' desk in Predevelopment. Instead, he was working in greater depth on microgravity programmes using sounding rockets and parabolic flights, the results of which directly informed the development of payload components for the future Spacelab missions. Then, in 1980, the TEXUS programme commenced, also under Fuchs' aegis, with rocket launches in Kiruna in Sweden. This programme is still highly successful today.

1981 would prove to be a significant year in Manfred Fuchs' career. At the beginning of the year, the government decided to consolidate the aerospace industry in Germany. First, MBB in Ottobrunn was to merge with ERNO. By then Manfred Fuchs had climbed high up the

30th September 1976

Manfred is appointed
Chairman of ASN

1976

He becomes a German
citizen

25th June 1978

Election as Chairman of the
M.E.S.H. consortium

corporate ladder. Many of the firm's successes would not have been possible without him. Indeed, his reference from MBB/ERNO would later read, "He used his outgoing personality to actively network and make contacts for our firm." It went on to state that "He performed his duties with exceptional creativity, personal commitment and extraordinary expertise and professional ability, including pioneering work without precedent." The chances were he would have risen even higher.

"Manfred always wanted to effect change. Not just in space, but in the party as well."

Ever since 1979, he had been becoming more involved in the Bremen CDU and, as the party's Deputy for Economic Affairs and Foreign Trade, he first attended to the development of the ports of Bremen and was soon writing the party's space policies. Fuchs struck up a close friendship with the then state party leader Bernd Neumann. "Manfred always wanted to effect change. Not just in space, but in the party as well. His principled dedication and immense optimism set him apart.

The success of the ARIANE rocket launch from Kourou spaceport, French Guiana, was a milestone in the history of European space flight.

24ᵗʰ December 1979

Maiden launch of the
European launch vehicle
ARIANE 1

Heinz Riesenhuber, Minister of Research and Technology from 1982 to 1993, visiting ERNO to learn about advances in space technology.

worked for almost ten years in long-standing Bremen coffee shop Café Jacobs. When Romana moved to Munich and Marco to Hamburg and Berlin, both to study law, Christa wanted to commit herself 100% to work, and to work for herself at that. She first considered opening a shop selling wool in the local shopping centre, but, after meeting the Otto family and after discussing with Manfred the prospect of working together, she embarked on the hydraulics venture. OHB's business was essentially building and repairing electrical and hydraulic systems for the German armed forces. When she took over the management of the small enterprise with 5 employees in the Hemelingen district of Bremen on 4th December 1981, Manfred was a silent partner at first. When it came to restructuring the ownership, stake acquisitions and the future direction of the firm, he was in the background pulling the strings. He had big plans for the business, as Ulrich Schulz, the first engineer at OHB, gathered during his job interview in 1982. When he set eyes on the small-time operation he wanted nothing to do with it, but then he met Manfred Fuchs. "He was a very charismatic man. He envisioned a creative troupe of between 100 and 200 people to ensure flexibility and innovation. The last thing he wanted was an outfit caught up in protocol, as was the case at ERNO. He said openly and candidly that things would be very informal at the start and that this would change over the years. He promised it would be exciting, and that was not an understatement."

'We've got to do something about that,' was one of his favourite phrases," the later Deputy Minister recalled.

It was in the Bremen CDU that Manfred met Mr and Mrs Otto. The owners of the small maintenance business Otto Hydraulik Bremen (OHB) wanted to retire and were looking for someone to take over. At the same time, Christa Fuchs was on the lookout for a new professional challenge. Before the children left home, the mechanical engineering entrepreneur's daughter had

1979

Deputy for Economic Affairs and Foreign Trade for the Bremen CDU

The early days of OHB in the Hemelingen district of Bremen

Manfred Fuchs had been toying his whole life with the idea of working for himself, especially since his whole family in South Tyrol were entrepreneurs. However, he used to tell most of his friends that his plans for retirement were a hotel in South Tyrol. When the opportunity arose in 1981 to take over the small venture OHB, his plans began to change. He and Christa talked about her getting things going and his coming on board a few years later, when the children had finished their studies and were financially independent. For Manfred Fuchs, OHB was undoubtedly Plan B to give him an out of MBB/ERNO if things took a turn for the worse after the merger.

But for the time being he continued to rise up the ranks. Having been appointed joint signatory and Chairman of the M.E.S.H. Policy Committee, he became director of the Predevelopment department for orbital systems, Spacelab, Columbus, ARIANE, TEXUS, MAUS and experiments on 1st October 1982. His success was bolstered by the second successful launch of the ARIANE rocket on 23rd May 1982. At the end of the year, on 8th December, Vallerani, Fuchs and Greger were honoured in Bonn by the German space agency (DARA) for their outstanding contribution to the bilateral collaboration between Italy and Germany that led to the construction of the European Columbus module. Spacelab took off on its first mission on board a Space

 4th December 1981

Christa becomes managing partner of Otto Hydraulik Bremen

 11th December 1981

Manfred is a member of the CDU's Federal Committee for Research and Technology

The TEXUS sounding rocket is one of the most successful programmes initiated by Manfred Fuchs.

Shuttle on 28th November 1983 and successfully spent eleven days undergoing tests in orbit, giving Manfred, the "spiritual father of Spacelab", and his team another notch on their belt.

Manfred pressed ahead with other matters. Although the reorganisation of MBB/ERNO meant that satellites would from then on be developed and built solely by MBB in Ottobrunn, ERNO began developing a national telecommunications satellite for the Federal Post Office, DFS-Kopernikus. Fuchs obviously did not care for the North-South divide that had been imposed, which was divesting his department of more and more competences, and fought it to the end. Leading the charge "to bring the satellite back to Bremen" was his employee Gerhard Schneider. Schneider noted, "I can only say that he was a huge support to me on DFS-Kopernikus. Manfred often swam against the tide. His goal at ERNO was always to grow the company. His chief motivation was not self-promotion but actually the firm's growth. He did a lot of groundwork for ERNO's business." In fact, DFS-Kopernikus was then completed under the leadership of the Bremen space division.

In May 1984, ERNO began building the Bremen-funded pollution control vessel "MPOSS" in an alliance with the Sarstedt shipyard and OHB. At this time, ERNO was increasingly bowing out of special technology

1982

Promotion to Director of Sales for orbital systems, launch systems and drives for MBB/ERNO

8th December 1982

DARA honours Fuchs, Vallerani and Greger for their role as co-developers of the Columbus programme

28th November 1983

Maiden Spacelab launch: the STS-9 mission successfully spends eleven days in orbit

projects. Whereas before they had been welcome in the interests of diversification, they were now removed from the new company's remit in the merger talks with MBB. For this reason, OHB later took over project leadership of the "Knechtsand" pollution control vessel and successfully oversaw the completion of "MPOSS".

As Christa and Manfred celebrated their silver wedding anniversary on 29th April 1985 surrounded by friends and family in South Tyrol, things at ERNO were not going Manfred Fuchs' way. The restructuring in the course of the merger did not serve him well. Predevelopment lost ARIANE, Spacelab, the Columbus module development and the satellite business. He was left out of the loop on important decisions. While before he had had autonomy and freedom to move within ERNO, the emerging hierarchies and the power struggle between North and South were increasingly cramping his style. "Manfred was highly influential. Spacelab became the main agenda and took priority in the company. Other players got in on the action and slowly but surely seized power over the firm. He was never one to take a step back, so he stepped away!" recalled Vallerani. Schneider concurred, "In the restructuring of MBB/ERNO, Manfred was not given the role he deserved, which was to take over the whole of Sales. And that encouraged him and his wife to embark on their own space endeavour."

"Knechtsand" and "MPOSS" are two pollution control vessels that were successfully launched thanks to OHB.

 May 1984

The "MPOSS" pollution control vessel is completed under the leadership of ERNO in conjunction with OHB and the Sarstedt shipyard

 4th December 1984

OHB registers the patent for the Raumkurier. Its inventors are Manfred Fuchs and Holger Stockfleth

Christa and Manfred Fuchs celebrated their silver wedding anniversary in Latsch. They renewed their vows before family and friends, who had missed out on the wedding ceremony the first time round.

On their silver wedding anniversary trip to Agadir, Morocco, in early 1985, Fuchs decided that it was time for him to work for himself. On 31st May 1985, at the age of 46, he left MBB/ERNO to start his career anew with his wife and their small enterprise OHB.

29th April 1985

Christa and Manfred celebrate
their silver wedding in Latsch

31st May 1985

Manfred leaves MBB/ERNO at
his own request

1985–
2001

Exploring new horizons

Christa Fuchs and her friend and business partner Sigrid Gäthje, shortly after taking over the as-yet small OHB.

In June 1985, Manfred Fuchs joined his wife Christa as co-managing partner of OHB. He had already seen to it that the company name was changed to OHB System in 1984. The addition of the word "System" gave a clue as to the direction he wanted to take the firm. The firm was still located in the Hemelingen area of Bremen. From 1983, Christa's friend Sigrid Gäthje had worked for OHB alongside her as a partner and authorised representative. The two of them took care of the finances while Manfred took over responsibility for the technical side after he came on board. According to

records, there were already ten people working for OHB System by then, almost half of them external consultants. Conditions in the company were basic and not particularly refined. It was down to Manfred Fuchs and his powers of persuasion and infectious optimism that anyone came to work for the firm at all, especially university graduates. Reinhard Stelljes' first impression was of "a workshop with a clay floor and machines which belonged in a museum". But then the charismatic Fuchs would step in and give a vivid account of his vision of a company with several hundred employees, flat hierarchies, lots of creative scope and the freedom to realise ideas. Given the industry status quo, his plans seemed a bit "out there", but he left no room for doubt that OHB and everything about it would change, improve and grow. The start-up phase involved plenty of hard graft and tasks outside the job description. He was honest about these circumstances. Plus, "he really did have a plan. Not like 'let's see where this road takes us.' He used to say, we'll start with MPOSS, then we'll get into experiments and hence space technology, then later we'll move on to bigger things, from the experiments module to the rack. But he also said, that's not set in stone. If the firm takes a different course because we have other ideas or discover other markets, we'll remain open to that possibility, too. That was the exciting thing about OHB System: he never limited activities to aerospace to the exclusion of all else," recalled Schulz.

1st June 1985

Manfred joins OHB as managing partner

September 1985

The Center of Applied Space Technology and Microgravity (ZARM) is founded

In 1985, OHB System's business was still predominantly service and repair work for the armed forces, as well as the development of an optical labelling

machine for Jacobs and development and systems work for the pollution control vessel MPOSS. In addition, OHB was Eberspächer's and Webasto's contractor for installing vehicle heaters. OHB had a truly motley array of orders on its books for the simple reason that it had to earn money to put the firm on a solid financial footing. This is where Manfred Fuchs' reputed pragmatism came into play again. While he had a clear idea of where he wanted to take the company one day, he also had the patience, the foresight and the modesty to work towards it step by step. In 1985, he also concluded agreements to work as a consultant for the space companies Kayser-Threde in Munich and MAN Technologie in Augsburg, and landed the first

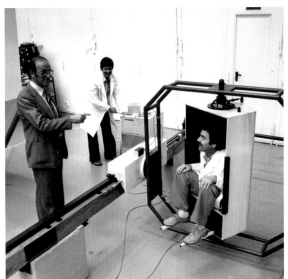

space projects for OHB. When a large German space company failed to deliver an experiment centrifuge for the D1 mission in Spacelab and the German Test and Research Institute for Aviation and Space Flight – DFVLR (today the German Aerospace Centre – DLR) revoked the contract, Fuchs saw an opening and put in a proposal to make the project a success. After more than 20 years in the space industry, his network was extensive and he had an established reputation as a reliable project partner. Together with his small team and without special expertise, he used imagination

In the beginning, Ulrich Schulz, the first engineer at OHB, had to apply himself to shipbuilding. Once Manfred Fuchs came on board in 1985, the work moved more and more into the field of space technology; for example, the Space Sled, in which Dr Peter Junk is getting comfortable in this picture.

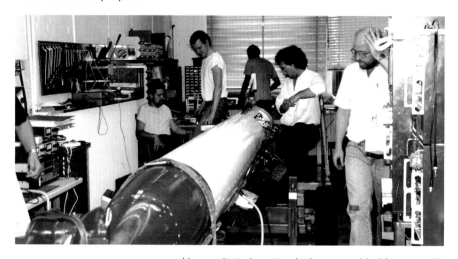

both the Federal Ministry of Research and DLR to fund this cost-effective form of microgravity research. "Manfred was a driving force. He used his political and business contacts to get his ideas realised. And he was able to inspire others. It was his great strength. He sometimes went on and on until whomever he was talking to agreed with him. He was able to fire them up. That was the secret to his success," said Gerhard Schneider.

MIKROBA was used five times in total in Kiruna, Sweden, under the leadership of OHB. Another mission was launched in China. Reinhard Stelljes recalled, "The experiments did not always go as planned. But that was never an issue because Professor Fuchs was an absolute master at finding the positive in every situation. 'We reached the target altitude. The parachute opened after the drop. We're heading in the right direction. At least, everything is working.' The word failure was not in his vocabulary." On the contrary: what every acquaintance mentions as one of his strongest characteristics is his fervent optimism. He was notorious for it. "If something did go awry, he simply justified it to himself. His optimism was boundless and he always said, 'Things will work out all right'. He brought people along with him. It was catching," said his daughter Romana. Gerhard Schneider added, "He was always confident that whatever he put his hand to would be a success!"

and ingenuity to invent a device assembled from standard parts which was subsequently made space-worthy. Its presentation, including all the tests, to the client ESA was a complete success. The concept of qualifying devices and components already available on the market for use in space, thereby bringing down costs, proved successful. Thus, through pragmatism and innovation, OHB System got a foot in the door with space agencies DLR and ESA, and its second project to boot: MIKROBA. According to Fuchs, the idea for this drop capsule came to him while he was brushing his teeth. The capsule with experiments on board would be dropped from a height of 40 kilometres and achieve weightlessness for around 60 seconds. He persuaded

May 1986

MIKROBA I mission

As Fuchs had planned, he now began to secure more and more space experiments. He knew politics and industry like the back of his hand and sought out niches where an as-yet-small firm like his could do business. For example, ERNO had a patent for an agitation tank, but the device was flawed. "So OHB and DLR came up with the idea of doing something else with it. We sketched a few ideas and this led to building a prototype and flying it on the KC135 to see how it behaved

"Professor Fuchs was an absolute master at finding the positive in every situation"

under microgravity," said Schulz. The tank performed perfectly during the parabolic flight in 1987 in Houston, Texas, but the project was discontinued due to budget cuts. However, the test flight went down in OHB history because Manfred Fuchs and Ulrich Schulz found something else to do during the two-hour wait at the airfield. "The plane took off, we sat down on two chairs and he said, 'Let's write the organisational chart.' There were maybe ten of us, so there was a lot of repetition of names on the chart," said Schulz with a grin.

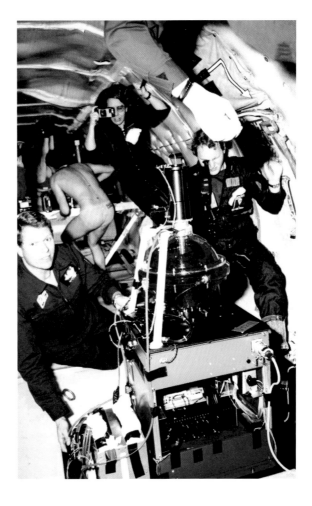

OHB employee Dirk Glander (right), filming agitation tank testing in parabolic flight over Houston.

10th June 1987

Agreement between OHB and NIS to operate the re-entry capsule TOPAS

1987

Parabolic flight with agitation tank in Houston, Texas

In the meantime, Manfred Fuchs' plans for OHB System and the news of his first moves to implement them had got around. Some of his former employees took the leap with him. One of them was Wolfgang Wienss, who had been responsible for "Transport Systems" in Predevelopment at ERNO. Alfred Tegtmeier, who had been in charge of "Payloads" followed him in 1987. Both were also close friends of Manfred Fuchs and lent OHB System a greater air of respectability because they were experienced space experts. More and more former ERNO employees joined OHB, including Dr Ingo Engeln, then a specialist in biological test set-ups, and Dr Peter Junk, who worked in the field of microgravity and was a project lead on the D1 mission. OHB System was slowly but surely acquiring a full complement of manpower and space expertise in the various areas. Without exception they all confirmed that they moved of their own accord, some because they, too, were dissatisfied after the merger, some because their characters and work methods better suited a small, flexible company with plenty of freedom. Peter Junk, for example, said, "I tolerate only two sorts of boss: those who let me do things my way and those from whom I can learn. Manfred was both in one!" The combative and critical Junk mentioned Fuchs' humanity in particular, "I have nothing negative to say about Manfred Fuchs. That sounds like flattery, but it's not: He was open to anything and everything. Back in ERNO I noticed that even when he was under stress, he always had a moment for whomever he met in the corridor – be it the cleaner or another manager. He was an incredibly sociable and great guy. With the prospect of such a boss, it didn't take long for me to decide to join him." Concerning his reason for moving, Ingo Engeln said, "Manfred Fuchs and I had the same philosophy: You have to do what's possible! You must progress according to your abilities and performance, not some formula or wishful thinking or careerism. That's the best way to advance. Maybe not as fast as others, but at least then you'll know what you've done and achieved!" Shortly before Christmas 1987, a significant event occurred. Manfred Fuchs announced en route to a supplier, "We're finally in the black!"

13th April 1988

MIKROBA II
mission

5th August 1988

COSIMA takes off on board
Long March 2 in China

The FALKE en route to its legendary test launch in France, where, after a successful mission, it landed on the roof of a shed.

"I tolerate only two sorts of boss: those who let me do things my way and those from whom I can learn. Manfred was both in one!"

The company was growing slowly but steadily. In 1988, OHB completed a contract for the electronics box for a protein crystal growth facility named COSIMA, which successfully went into orbit on board a Chinese launch vehicle that same year. Just like at ERNO, Fuchs established a broad base for OHB and worked in a consortium with Dornier, Kayser-Threde and ZARM (Center of Applied Space Technology and Microgravity) on the study for a reusable payload capsule RAUMKURIER, which would later give rise to the EXPRESS mission, which MBB/ERNO subcontracted to OHB for DLR. He subsequently embarked as main contractor on the development of the recoverable payload TOPAS for microgravity research (MikroG). He also did work in the area of space transportation systems, such as FALKE and COBRA. After Europe agreed to participate in the American Space Station (later the International Space Station ISS) in 1985 and after the Space Shuttle Challenger disaster in 1986, "it dawned on us that Europe had no suitable vehicles to prepare for zero-gravity experiments for this space station," wrote Fuchs in a press release at the time. MikroG was and remained one of his main occupations. He also campaigned for the construction of a drop tower in Bremen. His first ideas and notes on the subject dated back to ten years earlier. Talks gathered momentum after the Center of Applied Space Technology and Microgravity (ZARM) was founded at the University of Bremen in 1985. The head of the institute Prof. Dr Hans J. Rath wrote in a jubilee publication that he had actually intended it to be an environmental technology/hydraulic engineering institute. But then he met Christa and Manfred Fuchs. "This extraordinary couple

25th October 1988

Second place in the Schütting Prize

Dr Horst Binnenbruck (r), his assistant Quendler (l), Manfred Fuchs and Prof. Hans Rath at the ground-breaking ceremony marking the start of construction of the drop tower.

instantly impressed me. Together we managed to secure third-party projects in the area of environmental technology. We regularly met for project meetings, where Manfred Fuchs would try to convince me time and again to set up something in the area of space at the University of Bremen. Since I had been passionate about aerospace since I was a boy, I followed it up." Thus ZARM was born and the players got to work on the task of getting a drop tower built in Bremen. With similar commitment, Fuchs was also involved in bringing about a faculty of space at the University of Bremen, near which OHB System moved into the newly built red office building in Universitätsallee in autumn 1988. It had a garden, a pond and a long corridor flooded with light. "What he really wanted was to work in Bremen's central park. He had been to Silicon Valley and saw how the people spent almost their whole day walking in the park, but were never short of ideas. He believed people needed to be free to be creative," recalled Peter Junk. And Reinhard Stelljes added, "His vision was of spacemen as aesthetes, people who have to have room to think. They have to be out in nature; they have to see the world to clear their heads. His thinking really was far-sighted."

In his welcome address at the official opening of the new building complex on 18th November 1988, Fuchs pointed out that OHB, now a systems provider, had become a respected and feared competitor that was

18th November 1988

Inauguration of the new offices in the High-Tech Park, Universitätsallee 27

able to carry out small- and medium-scale space projects independently and intended to get involved in large-scale projects as a subcontractor.

OHB moved into its new offices in Universitätsallee, in the High-Tech Park in Bremen.

He had already had some success and so, in June 1989, he received the Hermann Oberth Gold Medal "for his huge contribution to German and European space research and technology; for his initiative in setting up his own company and for his patronage of the Hermann Oberth Society." He was also appointed Deputy Chairman of the society at the same time. That same year, the Bremer Landesbank selected OHB

System as the winner of its innovation competition and awarded it a prize of 50,000 Deutschmarks "for spotting a gap in the market for zero-gravity research, which the company filled with such activities as the Bremen drop tower, parabolic flight and drop capsules."

In 1989, the German space agency DARA began work in Bonn. It coordinated publicly funded space activities in Germany. Its Managing Director was Prof. Heinz

Honorary and Vice President of the Hermann Oberth Society Dr. Ing. h.c. August Friedrich, presenting the award to Manfred Fuchs.

24ᵗʰ June 1989
Hermann Oberth Society appoints him Deputy Chairman

25ᵗʰ June 1989
Presentation of the Hermann Oberth Gold Metal in Salzburg

In 1991, OHB was involved in 14 research projects for the German-Russian MIR '92 mission.

Stoewer, whom Manfred Fuchs knew from Bölkow (later MBB) in the 1960s. They started out as rivals and crossed paths again in the 1970s, when Stoewer took over as project lead on Spacelab for ESA. "Back then, Manfred already had form as someone with ideas and visions and the ability to develop relationships at a personal level that were special," said the present-day member of the Supervisory Board of OHB SE. At DARA – where Fuchs was Vice President of the Advisory Board – the two spacemen's working relationship intensified. "We did a lot together. It was the Columbus era. Manfred knew if we didn't have a decent utilisation programme, we wouldn't get the money or the political support to develop it for the space station. That was what spurred him on. He was thinking of the big picture." Manfred Fuchs became an important confidant and valued collaborator for Stoewer, but not just because of his vision and technical ability. "He had an honesty that was more than integrity. Honesty is more important because it implies consistency as well. He did what he said he would. It did not matter to him whether it was in the contract or not," said Stoewer.

The MikroG field at OHB System was doing well, with many new contracts for the D2 and MIR 92 missions as well as the preparatory work for the Columbus module. By around 1990, the company had grown to at least 70 skilled workers. Manfred began to expand the

1989
Foundation of DARA

26ᵗʰ October 1989
OHB wins the Bremer Landesbank innovation competition

1990

OHB is the main contractor for the D2 experiments Biolab and Anthrorack

1990
Commencement of development, analysis and design of SAFIR 1 (Satellite for Information Relay)

firm's activities further and set about breaking into satellite development. Peter Junk recalled; "We got into systems technology through manned space missions. And then Manfred said, 'The firm is big enough now for me to be able to go into satellites.'" To gain experience, Fuchs initiated the SAFIR project. Two small telecommunications satellites were developed and financed by OHB System. They made Manfred Fuchs, or rather OHB, the first private satellite owner in Germany, just like his grandfather Josef was once the first man in Latsch to own a truck. At the same time, OHB made another successful foray into satellite construction in conjunction with ZARM. For DARA they developed and built the scientific microsatellite BremSat, which successfully completed its mission. Then came subcontracts for the major European environmental satellite ENVISAT. Fuchs' plan to carry out smaller projects independently and larger projects as a subcontractor came to fruition. In this manner, he gradually built up OHB System's systems capability because "he was fully aware that, without it, he would remain a bit player. He did not want to become or remain a supplier; he wanted to stand on his own two feet. And that required systems capability," said Stoewer. Plus, he believed that, given the developments in microelectronics, satellites would no longer have to be as big as before. A long-standing trend in America, Fuchs caught up in Germany and Europe, filling a huge gap in the space industry. Of course, the

Model of a SAFIR satellite. OHB built two of them in-house to demonstrate systems capability in small satellites to the market.

6th September 1990

First and only Falke test launch in France. Development is discontinued because ESA terminates the Hermes programme

10th September 1991

Presentation of the Eugen Sänger Medal from the German Aerospace Society (DGLR)

The Columbus Hall is OHB's first large clean room.

large concerns were still interested in realising large-scale projects. So, these small satellites gave Fuchs a new domain, and he slowly gained acceptance for them using his excellent network.

OHB System again needed more space for its growing order book and ever-larger projects. The Columbus Integration Hall was inaugurated in 1993. Only two years later some of the around 170 employees moved into the new, white office building next door. However, there was a snag: Universitätsallee ended at his first office building and the second building "next door" was actually in Achterstrasse. Many a person would simply have lived with the inconvenience, but not Manfred Fuchs. He successfully applied to have Universitätsallee extended and paid for new stationery for the businesses affected.

At the same time as the move to the new offices in 1995, Marco Fuchs joined his parents' company. The law graduate and attorney-at-law started on a part-time basis. Manfred was already thinking about business succession and urged his children to think about joining OHB System. Romana was not interested because she was practising law in Munich and did not want to move back to Bremen. However, Marco was more open to the idea after his law firm in New York sent him back to Frankfurt. "I was never a lawyer through-and-through. The job was fine and varied, but

1st March 1993

Foundation of the telematics firm OHB Teledata

15th May 1993

Official opening of the Columbus Integration Hall

essentially you're just helping other people with their problems and wishes," said Marco Fuchs, revealing a strong independent streak. He also described how clever Manfred was in reeling him in. "My father made it easy for me. He offered me a part-time job and said, 'We're doing great, new things here you can take care of. It will pay your social security and you can move back to Hamburg. You just commute here two days a week, easy!'" No sooner said than done.

The "great, new things" referred to the foundation of OHB Teledata. The idea behind it was to forge new business fields using spin-offs: In this case, marketing satellite data for terrestrial applications such as vehicle tracking. In addition, OHB System started looking all over the world for businesses to acquire a stake in. It invested in the US communications satellite network ORBCOMM, founded a German representative for it and bought a stake in Carlo Gavazzi Space in Milan. "Manfred had always wanted to own something in Italy," said Ernesto Vallerani, who bought up a number of firms for Aeritalia to give it better control over the Italian space industry. Carlo Gavazzi Space was one of these firms. He offered Manfred an initial 50% stake in the company and the role of head of strategic development. Fuchs gratefully accepted. Today, Carlo Gavazzi Space is a wholly-owned subsidiary of OHB SE and goes by the name OHB Italia.

Model of the BremSat microsatellite.

Friends for life: Manfred Fuchs and Ernesto Vallerani.

"When I joined, the firm was in the process of becoming a group of sorts. Until then it was really just OHB System. So, at the beginning, I wasn't involved in the core business; more this new business development side," said Marco Fuchs, describing his start at OHB. Although he was the founder's son, he was not given preferential treatment and was installed at a small desk in a corridor because he was only there two days a week. He had no job description. It was up to Marco

3rd February 1994

Launch of BremSat aboard the Space Shuttle Discovery, one of the first German microsatellites and developed from 1990 by ZARM with OHB's involvement

4th November 1994

Launch of SAFIR I aboard the Russian Zenit-2 carrier rocket

23rd November 1994

Manfred Fuchs is named Honorary Professor at Bremen University of Applied Sciences and again shares a lecture hall with his friend Prof. Erich Overesch for the occasion

to come up with his duties. "That how we do things here!" was what his father said.

Manfred Fuchs was broadening the company's horizons with the addition of complementary business fields. In the process, relations with Russia deepened. Initial contact was made during the MIR 92 mission not long after the fall of the Iron Curtain. "They showed us

A young Angela Merkel visiting the upwardly mobile OHB with Bernd Neumann.

everything they had at the time. And then Manfred Fuchs simply bought a missile: a dummy without a propulsion system or nuclear warhead. The American secret service had spent 16 years trying to get a photo of the missile. And then there it was sitting in our yard. He knew very well that he could also hugely impress clients with things like that. And he had the contacts, of course! The news was out in no time. I don't know how many German chancellors and members of parliament we had here...," recalled Peter Junk. In the mid-1990s, Fuchs founded COSMOS International Satellitenstart GmbH. Talks about the purchase of launch services using the comparatively cheap Russian launch vehicle had already been under way for quite some time. Prof. Dr Indulis Kalnins came to OHB for the negotiations and to step up relations. He was impressed by one of the Russian project partner's visits to Bremen, "They say the Russians are very warm and welcoming. I'd say that Manfred Fuchs outdid them. We were invited to Manfred and Christa's home. He gave us a tour of the house. He even marched us through his bedroom. 'Here is my bathtub and the grandchildren sleep there.' It was something else." Next came an unannounced visit to Marco's house, followed by a slap-up meal in a restaurant. Manfred Fuchs' authenticity and pragmatism were hard to top. This led him to successes, such as the SAR-Lupe proposal, which had a considerable competitive advantage because of the cheap launch services.

1995

Moving into the new offices at Universitätsallee 29

Bremen University of Applied Sciences named him honorary professor for "Modern Space Systems" in 1994, praising his efforts to get students more involved in industry, for introducing a practical semester and for having facilitated many successful theses with MIKROBA. "To cap it all off, Mr Fuchs procured a research and development contract for the university, which led to the construction and testing of the first fully regulated cold gas propulsion system in the world by a development team seated in the mechanical engineering faculty," said Prof. Overesch in his address.

Meanwhile, OHB System was getting new work, as the company won the contract for the scientific satellite ABRIXAS from DLR. The X-ray telescope weighing almost 500 kilograms was not only a step up in size for the company, but was also an acid test. The mission failed because the main battery overheated in orbit. It was a bitter setback for the entrepreneur, who until then had been moving onwards and upwards. "I think it was the most difficult point in his career. He had to answer a few unpleasant questions from DLR and of his own. The strain was visible. Worry lines took the place of his trademark smile for some time," recalled Stelljes. Then came another loss-making large-scale project: the development and execution of the node for the International Space Station ISS ran over budget. "It was a tipping point for OHB, and the question was, would we fall by the wayside? Then came the dry spell.

Prof. Dipl.-Ing. Heinz-Hermann Albers, the then deputy rector of academic and student affairs at Bremen University of Applied Sciences, presenting the diploma awarding the title of Honorary Professor.

We were working at maybe 50% capacity, but nobody was made redundant. We all kept our jobs," recalled Reinhard Stelljes. On this subject, Marco Fuchs said, "Financing was incredibly difficult, hugely expensive, high interest rates, we debated long and hard. We put absolutely everything into it, including our private assets. If it hadn't worked out, we would have lost our homes." The fact that the Fuchs family were willing to

1995

Lawyer and attorney-at-law Marco Fuchs joins his parents' firm, initially on a part-time basis

The X-ray satellite ABRIXAS in OHB's clean room.

put their houses on the line was down to their firm conviction that the future was bright and also to "their loyalty to their employees. Unlike many managers today who hire and fire at the drop of a hat, Manfred felt more like a 'father' to the firm. The way he saw it, he was not only responsible for the figures and profit, but also for the people. He was devoted to the employees on a truly personal level because he needed this sense of family. There are lots of stories about how the Fuchs family helped out people privately," said Stoewer.

Manfred Fuchs did not let setbacks hold him down for long. Nor did he look for someone to blame within the company. "Every so often something went wrong," said Ingo Engeln, "but he wasn't in the blame game. His attitude was, 'If you don't try, you won't achieve anything.'" However, open and honest internal and external communication was always important to him. He believed that, to find a solution together, problems needed to be aired rather than brushed under the carpet. "That doesn't mean he disclosed everything, but he never said anything incorrect," said Engeln.

Fuchs worked flat out on a solution to extricate OHB System from its rut. When Germany decided it wanted its own radar satellite system for the armed forces in 1998, Fuchs wanted in. It was a large-scale project with an initial projected cost of two to three billion Deutschmarks, which far exceeded his firm's capaci-

March 1996

Nominated "entrepreneur of the year 1995" in Bremen (ASU: Independent Enterprise Working Group)

ties. He therefore entered into talks with the major tenderers to negotiate a certain amount of work for OHB, and was given the brush-off. Manfred Fuchs absolutely detested unfair treatment, so he did not accept the rejection. He decided to set up his own proposal team and take on the competition. "He was very friendly whenever possible. If his opponent turned nasty or seemed unwilling to find a solution together then his attitude was, bring it on, may the better man win!" said Ernesto Vallerani. Heinz Stoewer, too, recalled, "Manfred could be hard as nails sometimes. He would say, 'My way or the highway.' This was how it was with SAR-Lupe. There were a lot of decisions where he said, 'all or nothing'. And there were lots of decisions where he said, 'it's better to collaborate on this because then we can spread the risk. And others need to make a living too.' He always said that: 'others need to make a living too.'"

"If you don't try, you won't achieve anything"

It was a risky venture because, at that time, OHB had not quite 300 employees and was dwarfed by the powerful competition. Manfred Fuchs pulled out all the stops. He sought assistance from his friends and supporters in the Bremen Senate and in the ministries concerned. In the meantime, Dr Fritz Merkle from Carl

Zeiss AG had moved to OHB. The two men knew each other from their work in the German Aerospace Industry Association (BDLI) and from the ABRIXAS project, for which Zeiss supplied the telescope. Merkle was in charge of the "Military Optics" department amongst other duties and therefore had good, helpful contacts with the German Federal Office of Defence Technology and Procurement (BWB). He moved to OHB in what was a relatively uncertain time because he, too, was taken with Fuchs' charisma and he "found the start-up spirit, the enterprising mindset and the appetite for risk thrilling," said the physicist, who was now actively involved in preparing the proposal. Then Fuchs had another important encounter. He met the renowned radar expert Hans-Martin Braun, who, unlike the competitors, used the more stable and more sophisticated SAR technology. With him and his expertise on board, the proposal for the armed forces was drawn up. The project was given the title SAR-Lupe. In the end, a small team of about just ten people made the impossible possible. They came up with a visionary, redundant system comprising five small satellites and offered cheap launches using Russian Cosmos launch vehicles as well as operation of the satellites for a period of 15 years. "Our proposal was much more sophisticated and much cheaper," said Fritz Merkle. Heinz Stoewer added, "The way Manfred landed the SAR-Lupe contract; the way he organised the project, was amazing. He started a revolution with his constellation

July 1997

Presentation of the
Hermann Oberth Gold Ring

60

Two centrifuges for the biological research laboratory EMCS (European Modular Cultivation System) built by OHB for the American module of the International Space Station ISS.

of small satellites. This was 'New Space' in the truest sense of the word! However, I also remember a discussion we had about self-finance, bank guarantees and insurance. It was a very difficult trade-off that was fraught with risk. But he was prepared to take the risk, and it paid off!"

Manfred Fuchs would probably have replied to this with one of his favourite quotes, from the Austrian-German sociologist Helmut Schoeck, "The greatest risk in this day and age is the fear of risk." That said, he was never careless. Ernesto Vallerani put it thus, "Manfred was never afraid to take risks, but not because he didn't understand them. In fact, he considered them closely and knew he could overcome them with a sound approach."

While Manfred and the team were putting the finishing touches to the SAR-Lupe proposal, Marco Fuchs brought the telematics company OHB Teledata to an IPO in March 2001. He had wholly owned the company since 1998. He, Ulrich Schulz and Hans J. Steiniger from Apollo Capital Partners prepared the IPO, which brought in urgently needed capital. The collapse of the technology segment of the German stock market after 11th September 2011 was sobering at first. Nevertheless, the Fuchses made the best of the unfortunate situation and treated it as an opportunity to reposition themselves.

10th July 1998

SAFIR II mission on board Zenit-2

28th April 1999

Launch of ABRIXAS

1999

Manfred Fuchs is made Vice President of the Friends of ZARM and the Hermann Oberth Society

OHB's concept for the radar
reconnaissance system
SAR-Lupe wins the firm the
contract.

2001

Manfred Fuchs
becomes Chairman
of the SME Space
Alliance

13th March 2001

IPO of OHB Teledata
on Neuer Markt,
Germany's market
for technology
shares

When OHB received the official contract to build the SAR-Lupe system on 17th December, the mood was upbeat. Many of the big newspapers would soon report for the first time, but certainly not the last, about the incredible victory of David over the Goliath of the space industry. Change was in the air at OHB at the end of 2001. With perfect timing, the new, futuristic office building in Karl-Ferdinand-Braun-Strasse was completed, and to this day it is the company's headquarters and a symbol of the big break.

End of 2001

The new premises in Karl-Ferdinand-Braun-Strasse are completed in less than one year

17th December 2001

OHB is awarded the contract for the reconnaissance satellite system SAR-Lupe

2002–
2014

Conqueror of the skies

The environmental satellite ENVISAT was launched on the night of 1st March 2002. OHB's contribution was significant: from ground systems to on-board instruments.

Things started to look up for OHB in 2002. The Fuchs family managed to turn the crisis that brought about the collapse of Germany's market in technology shares to their advantage. They consolidated the listed OHB Teledata and OHB System, with its strong order book, under OHB Technology. "Our saving grace was the combination of the SAR-Lupe contract and the financial clout the IPO gave us. These two factors were equally vital, without a doubt. Without the money, OHB would have had no future. And without the SAR-Lupe contract in the bag, we would never have become a satellite systems provider," said Marco Fuchs, looking back.

This showed the symbiosis between the technical visionary Manfred, the business development strategist Marco and the financial expert Christa. She stayed in the background on technical matters, but she was very much in the fore when it came to corporate strategy, human resources and, above all, financial decision-making. Christa was seen as the tough businesswoman who held the purse strings and who "every so often brought Manfred back down to earth because his head was in the clouds," said Ernesto Vallerani. Then, on 6th July 2002, she, too, was presented with the Wernher von Braun Gold Medal in Garmisch-Partenkirchen by the international society promoting the space effort for her "fearless work building up OHB... in a particularly difficult environment".

20th March 2002

OHB Teledata and OHB System are consolidated under OHB Technology AG

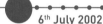

6th July 2002

Christa Fuchs is awarded the Wernher von Braun Gold Medal by the international society promoting the space effort

28th September 2003

Engineering Science Award from the International Academy of Astronautics

When OHB Technology was founded, Marco Fuchs took over company management. "When I officially became his boss and he my subordinate, he never railed against it, that I noticed. He was modest, he was always positive about it. I never really had any disputes with him," recalled Marco, who saw Manfred as his closest adviser and "often went to him for a confidence boost". Marco put the relatively harmonious handover of the reins down to their differing interests: "The IPO and the group were nothing special to him. My parents were concerned mainly with OHB System." While Marco was fine-tuning the European expansion strategy – by 2003, OHB Technology was already ranked first in Germany and tenth in Europe in the list of fastest-growing high-tech companies – Manfred continued building up OHB System's core business. He saw to the expansion of the systems capabilities both in terms of personnel and development and pressed ahead with many proposal activities and studies of missions such as Moon, Mars and Earth observation. He also represented the firm's interests on various committees; for instance, as Deputy Chairman of the Space Committee of the German Aerospace Industry Association (BDLI).

When the space division of MAN came up for sale in 2005, a family meeting was held and the decision was taken "to buy it based on a gut feeling", as Manfred Fuchs put it in an interview with Flugrevue magazine.

Of course, this description was an oversimplification but it showed the agility of the family-run company. The family's ability to meet in their offices in the

evening or at the weekend, if necessary, and decide in a flash what were often complex matters was credited to Manfred Fuchs. "He was extremely quick at making decisions. No red tape, no over-complication, forth-right... this is the problem, that's the solution. Done, time to move on!" said Vallerani on the subject. Heinz Stoewer added that Manfred's good gut instincts often helped him. "Some managers these days have to have all the facts and figures before they allow themselves to make a decision. It sometimes takes weeks, months or even years. The decisiveness that Manfred always

Start of work on the SAR-Lupe satellites in the new integration hall.

Marco Fuchs took over the company management in 2002. It was a happy occasion for his parents and sister, too.

2nd April 2004

OHB delivers the medicine laboratory EPM for the Columbus module of the ISS

28th May 2004

Official opening of the SAR-Lupe Integration Hall

November 2004

Foundation of Luxspace Sàrl

Former Mayor of Bremen, Henning Scherf, visiting OHB.

development of its predecessor, the Europa rocket. He had helped get the European launch vehicle off the ground, so to speak. Now, he was returning to his roots. For him, the purchase was akin to picking the fruits of bygone labours. "It was one of his babies, and now he was bringing it home," remarked Fritz Merkle.

Not only was Manfred reaping rewards, however; he continued to sow the seeds for the future as well. When the first SAR-Lupe satellite successfully went into orbit at the end of 2006, the ESA contract to develop a platform for "small" telecommunications satellites was in the pipeline by March 2007. This project, Small-GEO, was the product of years of personal dedication on Manfred Fuchs' part. One of his last tasks at ERNO was to advocate for the development and construction of the communications satellite DFS Kopernikus in Bremen. After that, there were no major activities in this sector in Germany. The country lost systems capability for geostationary telecommunications satellites.

had was part of the firm's success. In our complex business you can only know maybe half to two thirds of the facts. The rest you have to intuit. And Manfred was brilliant at it!" In purchasing MAN Technologie, Marco Fuchs and Hans J. Steininger, whose company Apollo Capital Partners acquired 30% of the business, had the OHB group's strategic growth in mind. For Manfred Fuchs, there was an element of nostalgia to the purchase. MAN Technologie (later MT Aerospace) was deeply involved in the ARIANE business. In his early years at ERNO, Manfred was instrumental in the

"His dream company didn't have 2,000 people – more like 200. Then he could get to know them all personally."

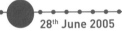

28th June 2005

OHB Technology and Apollo Capital Partners acquire MAN Technologie AG, Augsburg, and found MT Aerospace AG

6th October 2005

Prof. Fuchs receives the Laurea honoris causa in Ingegneria Spaziale, an honorary doctorate in space technology (Dr. h.c.) from the Polytechnic University in Milan

1st December 2005

Presentation of the AMW Award to Prof. Manfred Fuchs (Christa Fuchs also receives the award in September 2017)

Manfred Fuchs was known for his sense of duty not only to his company, but also to the space programme in Germany and Europe. For this reason, in 2004, he initiated and self-funded the LUX study to develop a new satellite platform for this purpose and engaged on all fronts to find acceptance with the space agencies and the political decision-makers. DLR got involved in the development from mid-2005 and the ESA added it to its long-term plan, investing in the platform as a separate element of the ARTES programme under the name ARTES 11. It was high time for Europe to reconquer the telecommunications market with innovative satellites. SmallGEO from OHB was the solution. "It was his thing, he was fully immersed in it," said Fritz Merkle. "Manfred Fuchs lobbied hard, first to the ESA and then at political level in Germany to ensure the country committed enough money and we retained systems leadership."

The size of the OHB group, which had been steadily built up by the family, was again a factor in this respect. At the end of 2004, the company Luxspace was founded in Luxembourg. When the country joined the ESA it was interested in co-developing SmallGEOs but had no companies operating in the field of space technology. OHB filled this gap and strengthened its position in the European project at the same time. Several more firms would join the OHB group over the course of the next few years; starting with the purchase of the

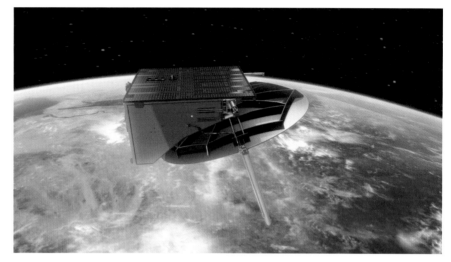

Munich space company Kayser-Threde, followed by the acquisition of a 100% stake in Carlo Gavazzi Space (OHB Italia) in Milan, Thales Alenia Space Antwerp in Belgium (Antwerp Space) and the space division of the Swedish Space Corporation (OHB Sweden). But more so, it was Marco Fuchs who deserved credit for this growth strategy. "I did it because I found it interesting from an economic point of view and because I felt a certain amount of pressure from the stock market. I also saw an opportunity to flex our muscles. Growing was not really his thing. His dream company didn't have 2,000 people – more like 200. Then he could get to know them all personally," said Marco.

The first of five SAR-Lupe satellites in total en route to the launchpad in Plesetsk Cosmodrome

19th December 2006

Successful launch of the first SAR-Lupe satellite

7th March 2007

OHB System wins the ESA contract for the SmallGEO satellite

On 23rd April 2007, an Indian
PSLV launched the AGILE
satellite built by Carlo
Gavazzi Space into space.
The procedure was organised
by COSMOS International,
OHB's launch services arm.

There were several reasons why Manfred nonetheless supported the development. Christa and he had handed over the reins to Marco bit by bit. While all the important decisions continued to be discussed by the

family – sometimes loudly and contentiously – Christa and Manfred Fuchs managed to achieve something in the end that very few company founders do: they gave their successor the freedom and time he needed to expand the company according to his vision. "I always admired how Manfred brought his son into the firm, supported him and was able to step back bit by bit to allow Marco to take on more and more responsibility. That is another of his life achievements!" said Heinz Stoewer, who followed the process closely in his capacity as member of the Supervisory Board of OHB SE. Besides, Manfred Fuchs was open to company expansion as long as it was likely to succeed. "Though expansion wasn't his core principle, nor was there any pressure to grow, he was always open to opportunities," said Ingo Engeln. Ultimately, Manfred Fuchs naturally wanted success and, for all his pragmatism, did like to show off his prowess.

His next opportunity to do so came in 2007, when the ESA and the EU put out a new call for tenders for the Galileo navigation satellite, after the project had ground to a halt. It was déjà vu for Manfred Fuchs. His OHB System was too small for the project size and he hoped to be a subcontractor. Fuchs approached the main tenderer with an offer to contribute one or two satellites to the project, and was turned down again. At the time, the successful SAR-Lupe project was drawing to a close. Fuchs asked project lead Ingo Engeln to

20th August 2007
OHB Technology AG acquires a
100% stake in Kayser-Threde
GmbH, Munich

10th April 2008
Appointed honorary
consul of the
Republic of
Kazakhstan
in Bremen

4th December 2008
Official handover of the
SAR-Lupe system to the
German armed forces

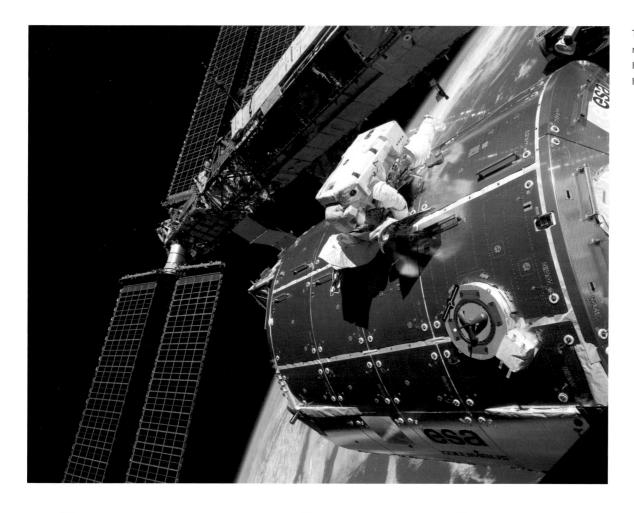

The European Columbus module docking with the International Space Station ISS on 11th February 2008.

18th June 2009

OHB System signs the contract with HISPASAT for the first SmallGEO mission H36W1

10th August 2009

OHB Technology AG acquires a 100% stake in Carlo Gavazzi Space S.p.A in Milan, Italy

27th August 2009

Christa and Manfred Fuchs are named honorary citizens and supporters of the University of Bremen

Artist's impression of a Meteosat Third Generation satellite, a large-scale project which OHB secured in alliance with Thales Alenia Space based on the development work on SmallGEO.

of Galileo satellites. "We fought fiercely for it. We had good concepts and made a good political pitch. In the end, we were more successful than we bargained for. We thought we would secure at least four or, who knows, maybe none at all. We got it so very wrong. In the end, we got 14 and the competitors none," said Engeln. Once again, just a small group of 20 people had made the next big step in the history of OHB. When the official contract was received on 26th January 2010, Manfred Fuchs retired from day-to-day business. In 2009, at the age of 71, he handed the role of CEO of OHB System over to the physicist Berry Smutny, whom he brought in to OHB from Tesat-Spacecom. The two companies had already had a long-standing successful working relationship. Smutny had made an outstanding contribution to the development of radar technology for OHB and its SAR-Lupe satellites. Fuchs became Chairman of the Supervisory Board and remained Chief Technology Officer of the parent company.

tender for the Galileo satellites. Manfred Fuchs instructed, "Secure one or two satellites! I don't care how!" Engeln was given free rein to put together a team to develop a technically and financially strong concept. Finding manpower within OHB was no easy task as the proposals for the large-scale projects SmallGEO and Meteosat Third Generation were being prepared at the same time as Galileo. Manfred Fuchs lobbied hard to get OHB System considered for a couple

"My father had become a bit weary by then and often had no interest in details any more. I was surprised when he suddenly had the discipline to leave work at a certain time in the evening. It didn't matter where he was or what was going on. He simply put down his pencil and went home to watch the 7 o'clock news. I do think he was happy with the transition; it was a load off," said Marco. But the contentment did not last long because Smutny caused quite a stir when the Norwe-

26th January 2010

OHB System wins the contract for the first 14 satellites for the European satellite navigation system "Galileo"

29th April 2010

Golden wedding anniversary

19th July 2010

OHB Technology acquires a 100% stake in Thales Alenia Space Antwerp in Belgium; the company name is changed to Antwerp Space N.V.

OHB won the contract for the Galileo satellites. The contract was initially for 14 satellites, then for a further eight and the ESA and the EC awarded the contracts for the final eight plus four spare satellites to OHB in 2017.

gian daily "Aftenposten" published "worrying statements", sourced from WikiLeaks documents, made by the new OHB CEO about the Galileo project. Fuchs was compelled to take action and avert damage. Smutny was relieved of all his duties at OHB in January 2011. His alleged comments went against pretty much everything that Manfred Fuchs represented all his life. At a board meeting on 15th July 2010, Fuchs stressed once again that OHB was a family company. Not only did that mean planning long-term, creating products that were a little bit better and more affordable than the competitors', making a profit and saving, but also treating one another well, fairly and with respect, both internally and externally. Aggression should not take the place of innovation, employees should be able to voice their opinion freely, have their grievances heard and be shown respect when they do so. "From partner to student on work experience, everyone is subject to the same company rules," he said.

OHB survived the WikiLeaks controversy almost unscathed, probably thanks in part to Manfred Fuchs' reputation for integrity throughout Europe. Now he had to appoint another successor and found the right candidate for the role of CEO of OHB System in his son Marco. From then on, Manfred sat on DLR and ESA committees as more of a figurehead and adviser. His reputation as a space expert was excellent and his achievements and services continued to be recognised

in the new millennium. In October 2005, he received an honorary doctorate in space technology (Dr h. c.) from the Polytechnic University in Milan in honour of the fruitful collaboration between Italy and Germany over the years and the partnership between the Polytechnic University and the Milanese company Carlo Gavazzi

2010

The Fuchs family buys Annenberg Castle

26th June 2011

OHB Sweden is founded as a result of the purchase of the Space Systems division of Swedish Space Corporation

Manfred received the Werner von Siemens Ring surrounded by family, friends and associates: Christine, Romana and Romed Fuchs, Bernd Neumann, Manfred and Christa Fuchs, Prof. Dr Joachim Ullrich (Chairman of the board of the foundation), Harald and Michael Fuchs, Alexander von Egen and Marco Fuchs.

Space, which Manfred Fuchs developed into Italy's top SME in the space industry. At the end of 2005, the Management and Economic Research Working Group (AMW) at Bremen University of Applied Sciences went one better and awarded him the AMW Award for his tremendous success in business. Prof. Erich Overesch gave the address for his friend, whom he had known for 45 years by then, and remarked that the secret of his rise was "his astoundingly serendipitous balance of head, heart and hand". "These are the wellspring of

13th December 2011

Presentation of the Werner von Siemens Ring

26th April 2012

The consortium comprising Thales Alenia Space and OHB System is selected to build the six Meteosat Third Generation (MTG) satellites

his success; his ability to realise products whose practicality and feasibility he believes in. In this, he is helped by his immense creativity and strategic competence. He exudes absolute reliability and great composure. He wins people over, both personally and professionally, with his unshakable optimism, his remarkable humanity and his amiable South Tyrolean charm."

"He wins people over, both personally and professionally, with his unshakable optimism, his remarkable humanity and his amiable South Tyrolean charm."

In 2008, his home town of Latsch, "in recognition of his huge services to science, business and mankind" gave him the freedom of the town and the Republic of Kazakhstan appointed him honorary consul. One year later, the University of Bremen named Manfred and Christa Fuchs honorary citizens and supporters in gratitude for ten years as endowed professor and for their unstinting patronage.

Marking Manfred's appointment as honorary consul of the Republic of Kazakhstan are Prof. Erich Overesch, Christa and Romana Fuchs.

On 13th December 2011, Manfred Fuchs received the highest award for technical sciences in Germany, the Werner von Siemens Ring, "in recognition of his success in advancing application satellite technology, putting Germany at the forefront of this field in Europe" and joined an impressive list of greats in the history of German technology alongside Wernher von Braun and Konrad Kuse before him. One year later, South Tyrol awarded him the Grand Order of Merit in acknowledgement of his services to the province. Manfred had

4th May 2012

Official opening of the Galileo Integration Hall

18th March 2013

Council of European Aerospace Societies (CEAS) Gold Medal awarded to Manfred Fuchs

Manfred's services to his homeland were recognised by the bestowal of the Grand Order of Merit of the province of South Tyrol.

achieved everything that was important to him. When he quite unexpectedly passed away following a heart attack at his holiday home in Altenburg, Caldaro, South Tyrol, on 26th April 2014, he could rest assured that his son Marco would continue his life's work and that his two native countries would commemorate both him as a person and his work in fitting fashion.

2nd July 2013

Contract for the SAR-Lupe follow-on system SARah

5th September 2013

Presentation of the "Grand Order of Merit of the province of South Tyrol"

26th April 2014

Manfred Fuchs passes away following a heart attack in Altenburg, Caldaro, South Tyrol

The visionary

World-renowned foresight

"A vision is the imagining of a certain state of being in the future; in other words, a picture of the future that is innovative and points the way forward."

Manfred Fuchs was often described by his associates and business partners as a visionary. He might not have been like Elon Musk, Larry Page or Mark Zuckerberg, who became billionaires almost overnight and today are involved in space flight with their visions of Mars colonisation and travelling to Alpha Centauri, the double star system 4.34 light years away, but, like them, Manfred Fuchs was always in search of groundbreaking ideas. He also had a vision of colonising the Moon, but he went about achieving his grand, distant goal with caution and within the bounds of his capabilities. He was more of a pragmatic visionary who set goals he could reach. As was so often the case in the space industry, projects took a long time to get off the ground. Manfred Fuchs had enough patience and stamina to achieve his goal little by little. "My father was capable of focusing on what was possible at that specific moment in time. It was truly amazing. For example, when we were designing a little PCB, he could visualise the next stages of development up to the entire space station and beyond, to the Moon," said Marco about his father's foresight.

His main driving force was the essential questions that preoccupied him all his life: "Where do we come from and where are we going?" He liked to discuss these questions in detail with his associate and friend Erich Overesch. The two men came at the subject from different perspectives. Roman Catholic deacon Erich's motivation was presumably more spiritual in that he wanted to know if there was a higher power, while Manfred's motivation was more scientific in that he wanted to explore the vastness of the universe by means of space technology to discover and understand its origin and evolution. Another factor was the assumption that humankind would have to leave Earth at some point in the distant future. "That is a fundamental belief that most of us have. There is life somewhere out there and, in the long term, we have to try to find it," recalled Heinz Stoewer from his private conversations with Manfred Fuchs. In his professional life he was first and foremost a visionary and in the industry he was regarded as an expert for his ideas and his pioneering, realistic perception of the space programme. However, he had clear goals in his private life as well.

He grew up in Latsch in an environment that did not satisfy his early interest in advanced technology. It was for this reason that Manfred decided, at the tender age of 13, to get the technical education he would need to pursue his aspirations. His path took him from Bolzano to Munich and finally to a course in aero-nautical engineering in Hamburg. That whole time he was driven by the need to understand the ins and outs of the subject of his fascination: aeronautics and later space flight. In ERNO's start-up phase, when the industry was still in its fledgling stage, he was able to give his ideas free rein. In Predevelopment he enjoyed some tremendous successes because he was always far-sighted enough to identify the needs of the clients and of the market; indeed, in some cases to create demand.

Prof. Erich Overesch said the mass celebrating Christa and Manfred Fuchs' golden wedding anniversary in South Tyrol. The two men were best friends and liked to discuss the philosophical questions "Where do we come from and where are we going?"

At the tender age of 13, Manfred Fuchs (standing directly in front of the blackboard) left his home town of Latsch and went to Bolzano to realise his dream of getting a technical education.

From the outset, his visions for space flight were very broad in scope. The first time he drew on all his skills was when the Americans started up the post-Apollo programme under President Nixon in the very early stages of space flight. The Americans were behind the Russians in the space race at that time and Manfred realised that they needed a break to regain respect internationally. Europe's proposal to use the Spacelab research facility on the Space Shuttle gave them their break. Manfred hit upon the necessity to first test and create the right conditions for astronauts to live in space. Thus, Spacelab was not only a test module for future space stations for the applied space technologies of manned space flight but, moreover, Europe was able to offer the Americans a civilian purpose for their Shuttle. With resolve and drive, Manfred Fuchs managed to win over all the decision-makers, especially in Germany, and ultimately obtained the Americans' approval.

When Manfred came up with the idea for Spacelab, there were initially only a few supporters in Germany and Europe. But he thought ahead and made the case for Spacelab. He knew straight away that "if we didn't have a decent utilisation programme, we wouldn't get the money or the political support to develop it for the space station," recalled Heinz Stoewer. For that reason, as well as large-scale projects like ARIANE, Spacelab and application satellites, Manfred aspired to establish smaller projects which were scientific in nature or paved the way for the colonisation of space or involved basic research. For example, microgravity research and the related experiments were very important to him. He worked very intensively in and promoted this area. He set up the Spacelab utilisation working group ASN and brought all the prospective customers and interested parties to the table. Manfred had a way of getting people excited about manned space flight and his visions. His approach was very clever; expanding the research potential by way of sounding rockets and drop capsules, which, though they created microgravity for only short lengths of time on their flight paths, cost substantially less. Under him, Predevelopment was very successful in this whole area, both in the development of experiments and in the planning, execution and evaluation of the results of the mission.

He always had his eye on the big picture, far into the future. He foresaw the space station being just a stepping stone to manned missions to the Moon and, one day, to Mars. Of course, in the Spacelab era, this was an even more distant prospect than now, but this development formed part of Manfred Fuchs' vision from early on. In that respect, he's not so different from today's high-flyers in the space industry, just that Manfred took smaller steps, which was probably due partly to the times he was in and the sometimes

quite tight budgets. He didn't have an unrealistic or impractical approach; quite the contrary. He was always thinking about feasibility, about the real probability of success, both short-term and long-term. He systematically and steadily worked in some areas – like microgravity research – for decades and was involved in their gradual realisation.

The constant expansion of space flight activities in Bremen is another example of this. Manfred realised early on that space flight and the advancement of technology had to go hand in hand. For that, what was required was a sort of "Silicon Valley", which so impressed him on a visit to the USA. In the beginning, only two space businesses were located in northern Germany: ERNO and later OHB. Today, thanks partly to his dedication, there are other institutes and enterprises in the industry as well as education and research activities which elevate the small city-state to a centre of space flight. This goes to show that he was an exemplary forward thinker who was quick to spot new directions and, especially, where they would

The Development Fixture test bench was built at ERNO in 1976 to ensure that everything subsequently ran smoothly at Spacelab.

lead. Not only that, he embraced them and had the vision to incorporate them into a viable strategy and then had the practicality to see them through to the end. One need only fit together the pieces of his career for it to become clear: the single-mindedness and continuity of his work were two key elements in his success!

"Manfred could tell you how you wanted your coffee. And then you'd wonder why you'd always had it black before."

Many of his work associates described him as someone with an extraordinarily curious mind. He was always willing to kick-start novel projects. One could say he assimilated everything around him – from the technical possibilities to the clients' needs – and transformed them into ideas. "We've got to do something about that," was a much-feared phrase of his, because he was stubborn and possessed formidable powers of persuasion. In the end, one came round to his point of view and had at least the same level of enthusiasm for his ideas as he did. "Manfred could tell you how you wanted your coffee. And then you'd wonder why you'd always had it black before," remarked Marco.

Manfred Fuchs never stopped setting new goals, including and quite especially when OHB came along. Even when he was still working for ERNO, he had a clear vision of what the small five-person operation would become. He vividly described the future of the

He gained a reputation as the mastermind of the Space Shuttle laboratory at the beginning of the 1970s.

Bremen's "Silicon Valley": Manfred Fuchs played an active part in developing the Technology Park (left) and attracting research and science facilities to the location.

Manfred Fuchs was able to
envision an up-and-coming
space company in these OHB
premises. He was able to sell
his vision to many people,
who took the leap with him.

Manfred Fuchs blazed a trail for the emergent market in small satellites. BremSat was the first.

company to Ulrich Schulz, the first engineer, who the Fuchses employed in 1982: a staff of at least 200, most of them university graduates, would give their creative and innovative ideas about space flight free rein in offices in Bremen's largest park, the Bürgerpark. This contrasted with the pathetic, run-down workshop in which Ulrich Schulz did his interview, a building that was almost impossible to find because only one unimposing sign indicated the existence of the firm. Manfred was open and candid that they would have to roll up their sleeves to get there, but that it would be worth the work. His charisma and his clear vision convinced Schulz, who still to this day does not regret having placed his trust in Manfred. Apart from the office building in the park, for which no one on this Earth would have obtained planning permission, his predictions and promises came true exactly as foretold and, eventually, were even far exceeded.

Certainly, Manfred's greatest achievement at OHB was his vision for satellites, which pointed the way forward. At a time when the major players in the industry were thinking of ever bigger satellites and dismissed any alternative as being purely academic, Manfred and OHB had a strict policy of developing small satellites. On the one hand, he was carving out a niche where he could fly below the radar of the large corporations and build his own empire. On the other hand, the technology was so far advanced that the trend was towards miniaturisation as it was. Manfred Fuchs and his team gradually increased their knowhow, starting with the University of Bremen-built small satellite BremSat, to the telecommunications satellites SAFIR 1 and 2, and on to their big success with SAR-Lupe, the reconnaissance satellite system for the German armed forces, which gave OHB its big break and emphatically confirmed Manfred Fuchs' vision.

A vision becomes reality: Spacelab was fitted in the Shuttle in August 1983 in the Kennedy Space Center. Its launch that November marked the beginning of manned European space flight.

Step by step, OHB systematically developed increasingly complex satellites. The company/the Fuchs family even owned its own communications satellite: SAFIR 2 (shown here with engineer Frank Ellmers).

It is thanks largely to his wife and business partner Christa that his countless ideas did not get out of hand and lead him astray. She would often rein him in with the financial argument when he was about to launch himself with unbridled enthusiasm into something that had the potential to get out of control or fail. "Just leave it be, Manfred," were his wife's cautionary words in such instances. They made an excellent team at the head of OHB, which they managed jointly.

Manfred had the same foresight in his private life. He knew where he wanted to be one day and had the stamina to take it one step at a time. When he bought a terraced house in Bremen, he informed his family that a detached house was on the cards in the foreseeable future, which he would then extend bit by bit to make it more comfortable. According to his daugh-

Manfred Fuchs liked fine things and prestige. Over the years he extended the house he owned in Bremen into a villa. This had been his plan from when he was still living with his family in a terraced house.

ter Romana, from when he was a child, he had dreamed of one day owning Annenberg Castle atop the mountain opposite his house and of which he had a full view from his room. Perhaps there's a bit of legend-building going on there, but it doesn't detract from Manfred's visionary status. He even planned his company's succession with similar foresight. Manfred slowly but surely withdrew from the business – which does not always happen in family firms – and before his death handed over full responsibility to his son Marco, and OHB is now bigger and stronger than ever.

Just like the Hubble Telescope, Manfred Fuchs liked to
look into space (the picture
shows the Tarantula Nebula
in the Large Magellanic
Cloud, a satellite galaxy of
our Milky Way), and wanted to
explore it. The manned
conquest of space inspired
his ideas all his life.

The man from South Tyrol

The man from the mountains

Manfred's grandparents Anna and Josef (seated behind the table), with their children Berta and Josef (front) and Luis, Helene, Rudolf, Romedius, Willy, Hans and Martin.

Meaning of the family crest from 1616: The fox is said "to play dead for the birds (ruling powers) in order to ambush them." The helmet represents nobility/special merit. The colour silver symbolises purity, wisdom, innocence, chastity and joy, while red stands for patriotism.

16 Fux 16

Manfred Fuchs was South Tyrolean through and through – on that we can all agree! However, what does being South Tyrolean mean? He was born and grew up in a valley surrounded by the mountains south of the Alpine divide. The province of South Tyrol is spread over an area of 7,400 square kilometres, of which just 6% is in any way inhabitable. The people who live there have to be resourceful and industrious to survive at all. The Fuchs family has been there since the 13th century and the surname is quite common. Until the mid-19th century, the economy of the region was dominated by mountain farming, hand craft and mining. From 1850 onwards, the timber, textile and food industries gradually developed. Manfred's ancestors were involved in this development from the start. For instance, Josef Fuchs, the progenitor of the Forst side of the family, took over a small brewery in 1863 and built it up together with his wife Filomena. Today, the Forst brewery is run by the fourth generation of Fuchses and is one of the largest breweries in Italy. The brewery has thrived down through the years under female leadership, which is unusual for the patriarchal and Catholic society. There was nothing unusual about it for Manfred, however, whose mother Paula also had a strong personality.

Her father Konrad Laimer came from a mountain farm in St. Pankraz in the Ulten valley, but, unable to find work there, moved to the market town of Lana, south of Merano. In Lana he operated a small sawmill with a cabinetmaker's shop. He married Amalia Rohregger from Eppan in 1911. They had four children together. Konrad died young in 1923 of unspecified causes and left his widow penniless. Consequently, she had to give up two of her children, Irmgard and Adalbert, to a family in Bolzano. Amalia moved to Latsch in 1925, presumably with her two remaining children Konrad and Paula, where an acquaintance of her deceased husband, a fruit seller named Zuegg from Lana, had found her a place to live. There Amalia met Josef Gerstl, who was 14 years her junior, and married him in 1929. Since they had no children, she adopted Kurt, the illegitimate son of Paula, who returned from Padua in 1937. The three of them lived together opposite Manfred's parents in the Moos area of Latsch. Amalia did not die until 1967, so Romana and Marco got to know their great-grandmother and enjoyed spending time with her during their visits to South Tyrol. "All of them called her simply 'Mother'. She was a kind, gracious and tall woman," recalled Romana.

The progenitor of the Latsch side of the family was Peter Paul Anton Fuchs, whose profession, unfortunately, is undocumented in the family history. However, one of his descendants was Manfred's grandfather Josef, a landowner who also had a sawmill, schnapps distillery and the guesthouse "Zum Hirschen". He and his wife Anna Gamper had 14 children. "The siblings were all entrepreneurs: one was in tiles, another was a miller, yet another had a bakery, one a large mill and another made roofing shingles," said Manfred's brother Romed, who took over and expanded their father's small transport business. The Fuchses are all described as inventive, resourceful and good with machines.

Industry, self-reliance and entrepreneurship evidently run in both sides of Manfred's family. The fact that he began his career as an employee was solely down to his passion, his line of work and his provider instinct. At that time, aerospace was still in the fledgling stage and the vast majority of the contracts were large-scale publicly funded projects. Secondly, he had a family to provide for when he was just barely in his twenties, so he wanted financial security. Thirdly, as Manfred mentioned time and again, he was afforded a great deal of autonomy and freedom at ERNO. Only after that

Manfred's ancestors:
wedding photo of his parents
Paula and Romedius and the
staff of his grandfather
Josef's sawmill on an outing
to Martello in 1906.

changed and his children were on their feet did he start his own business in his mid-forties. Despite being the first of his family to go to university and even though his job made him at least as successful as his relations who had their own business, the fact that he was an employee obviously bothered him. At any rate, he brought it up again and again in interviews and in conversations with friends. "A Fuchs from South Tyrol should be his own boss!" he used to say.

It is also worthwhile mentioning that the province has had a chequered, militant history marked by a struggle for autonomy and this has shaped the South Tyrolean character. The county of Tyrol belonged to the Habsburg Empire for over 550 years. When the monarchy collapsed in 1918 at the end of World War I, Italy obtained the territory in the south of Tyrol as far as the strategically important Brenner Pass. This pact violated the people's right of self-determination, a principle that the victorious powers had agreed to adhere to. South Tyrol nonetheless became a military protectorate and a policy of intensive Italianisation was introduced. The German and Ladin languages were repressed and even prohibited at times. Italian families were settled in the provincial capital Bolzano. In 1939, Hitler and Mussolini reached what was called the Option agreement, under which native German speakers were given the choice to emigrate to the German Reich or remain in South Tyrol but relinquish their German language and culture. The Option opened up a deep rift in the province. Although 166,000 people – or some 86% of the population – took up this Option, in the end only 75,000 emigrated and they returned home shortly after the end of World War II. They had hoped that all of Tyrol would be reunified, but this did not come to pass. Italy did promise its most northerly province autonomy in 1946 but progress was so slow that large sections of the population fought for self-determination from then on. The South Tyroleans therefore not only have a head for business, but are a proud, confident and freedom-loving people.

Manfred Fuchs was born into this cultural duality: he grew up knowing that despite being South Tyrolean he lived in a Romance country and had to make the best of the situation. What was he to do: struggle or surrender? Neither! "My father's generation was the first to embrace Italy. He, Romed, Sepp and all the others were the first opportunists who said, 'We're OK with how things are. We just have to learn the language, then we can do good business'," said Marco. Of course, at home, Manfred had been brought up to be tolerant and open-minded. And from his mother he had learned Italian – which was more intensive tuition than his fellow pupils got – and, in her bar, how to interact with people of different ethnicities. So, when Manfred went to Bolzano at the age of 13, he was well prepared for the bilingual capital of South Tyrol. "The unfamiliar did not scare him – he took it in his stride. This also explains his interest in the world in later years," said Marco. Given the province's turbulent past, it's no surprise that Manfred Fuchs had a lifelong interest in not just South Tyrol and its people, but also world history, the movement of borders, kingdoms and empires. "One gift that always went down a treat with my father was a historical atlas," recalled Marco. With almost childlike fascination he devoured films about Alexander the Great, Napoleon, Kublai Khan and the Inca kings. "When we were on holiday, he always bought an old coin, authentic or not. Even fragments of artefacts caught his eye," said Romana.

Nor is it surprising, in light of South Tyrol's history, that Manfred Fuchs developed a strong desire for fairness, honesty and a keen distaste for theft. He was known as an extremely calm and collected character

Manfred's grandmother Anna Gamper (left) chatting with an aunt of his while they weave. Even as a child, Manfred pricked up his ears to hear what they were talking about.

Romed's partner Dr Edith Götsch with her daughter Alexandra at one of the cabin parties in Martello valley.

Class reunions: Manfred was a regular at the
Class of 1938 reunions, and once said, "For
our 80th we'll all go to the moon – on me."

who rarely lost his temper, but when he did, one of
these was usually the cause. When Romana and
Marco once stole a couple of Lego bricks they didn't
have at home from preschool, Manfred used very
strong language. "Theft was an absolute no-no for
him. He said to us, 'I shall chop off your hands if you
ever steal again'," recalled Romana, who described
her upbringing as quite laid-back otherwise.

Life in Latsch shaped Manfred's personality in many
other ways. He came from relatively meagre financial
circumstances and grew to be industrious, frugal and
down-to-earth. Even when he was head of the company
he was never above getting coffee for clients or setting
up at trade fairs.

From an early age he showed one other trait that
would be invaluable later on in life as well: he was a
good listener. As a young boy, he often played in the
garden. Sometimes his aunts sat outside on the bench
and shared the latest village gossip. One day the topic
of conversation was an illicit affair, which was not suitable for children's ears. "Shush! He's listening!"
warned one of the aunts. However, the other one
thought it was safe for her to continue because the
young boy seemed to be playing away deep in concen-
tration. And so he heard every detail. Manfred Fuchs
liked to tell this anecdote to his employees. It was his
way of letting them know that he took in everything
that was going on around him even when he appeared
indifferent. This curiosity, coupled with his ability to
see information in broader contexts, was a factor
behind his success.

Although Manfred's profession had taken him to Germany at a young age, he never neglected his close ties
to his homeland. Far from it: he took at least two holidays in South Tyrol every year, either in the apartment

in Latsch, in his log cabin by the reservoir in Martello valley or later in the manor in Altenburg, Caldaro, or in Annenberg Castle, which he bought in 2010. However, the cabin was the hub. There, Manfred's friends and family from Germany and South Tyrol met every year for what was dubbed the "men's hike". After celebrating in style, the group used to go hiking. Their destination was often the highest peak in the area, the Ortler, at almost 4,000 m. The arduous climb culminating in a breathtaking view or perspective at the top is also a metaphor for Manfred's career. Hikers need patience and stamina to make it to the top. It was an important lesson for life that his homeland taught him.

It became tradition to hold what became known as the "cabin party" – started up by Manfred – at the same time as the hikes. For him, socialising and hospitality were basic human requirements that he had developed as far back as the time of his mother's bar. The grand party took place on Ferragosto/Assumption Day on 15th August, and Romana still continues the tradition today. Getting together all of the people he loved best from both "worlds" and wining and dining them was an important part of his private life. Everyone has a vivid memory of the parties in the basement bars and the riotous birthday parties in Huchting but especially the big parties in South Tyrol.

Christa and Manfred Fuchs also celebrated their silver wedding anniversary in Latsch. After 25 years of marriage, they renewed their vows, this time in a church ceremony. A bus was organised for friends from Bremen. The Fuchs family's parties were always well organised and they were generous hosts. The festivities went on for days and there was even a parallel programme to enable guests to see Manfred's homeland. Not only was he deeply rooted in South Tyrol and proud of where he came from, he also had a desire to

Rudi Sell, Erich Overesch, Manfred Fuchs and Manni Sendko taking a break on one of their hikes.

Having a drink with his oldest friend: Sepp Rinner and Manfred Fuchs knew each other since preschool.

In 1863, Josef Fuchs took over what was then a small brewery. Today, Forst is one of Italy's largest breweries, and is run very successfully by the fourth generation of Fuchses.

Every party was special: Raising a glass with the then governor of South Tyrol, Luis Durnwalder, and feasting at the Fuchs' cabin party.

promote it, advance it and give something back to it. His friend Sepp recalled something that Manfred said: "Now that I'm making so much money, I want to give back to Latsch." In the pizzeria of the local swimming pool, the pair very matter-of-factly discussed the sometimes substantial investments.

Margherita Fuchs von Mannstein, managing partner of the Forst brewery in Merano, also remembered her distant cousin as an extremely open person who was always very active: "He supported South Tyrol and did a lot of good deeds. And he had a vision for South Tyrol: a haven for scientists; a centre of thinking and research. He thought the landscape, the stillness, was perfect for it. He believed it would do the province good, as it would make it much less dependent on industry. He brought this up in his speech when he was given the freedom of Latsch. I found that passage just brilliant."

Thanks partly to his dedication, for instance, there is a satellite receiving station on the Horn of Renon near Bolzano today. Together with his Milanese company, he designed and built the service station for the European Academy Bozen/Bolzano (EURAC) to use satellite data to improve disaster control and environmental policy in his homeland.

Manfred's friend Sepp, who was the one who had nominated him for the freedom of Latsch, a motion which was unanimously passed, said, "Only two people have received the freedom of Latsch – it's not something we hand out every day." By way of thanks, Manfred donated the Robert Scherer stained glass window on the north wall of the Nikolaus church in Latsch. In addition, he initiated the unique Max Valier satellite project for school pupils in conjunction with the then governor of South Tyrol Luis Durnwalder. The aim of the project was to enable his alma mater, the Max Valier College of Technology, to design and build its own satellite. Manfred Fuchs felt very attached to his college and provided both financial assistance and manpower – in the form of OHB experts – to the project. He didn't live to see the launch, but the first sign of life from the satellite came on 23rd June 2017 with the transmission "MAX VALIER SAT TNX MANFRED CHRISTA FUCHS".

"He had a vision for South Tyrol: a haven for scientists; a centre of thinking and research."

School principal Barbara Willimek said, "The things he believed in, he simply made them happen. He let nobody stand in his way. It was no different with our satellite. There were a few critics who said we couldn't do it but he always believed in us and supported us. He was always there when problems arose, and came up with the solutions. Both Christa and Manfred Fuchs are truly inspirational people." His friend, the South Tyrolean businessman and lawyer Alexander von Egen, added, "The satellite project was a wonderful idea. He used to say that the youth should be nurtured for they are the future!"

He was always a homebird at heart. Born in South Tyrol, he remained South Tyrolean and became an advocate of all Tyroleans. He offered the hand of friendship to his homeland. It was always nice when Manfred was there. "When he and Christa were in South Tyrol, they stayed either in their modern apartment in the centre of Latsch, with a view over the rooftops, which they did mostly in the winter months, or in the log cabin in the mountains. Or rather, they used to

Manfred Fuchs is one of the very few people to have been given the freedom of Latsch.

Raising the flag of Bremen outside the cabin in South Tyrol.

The stunning view from the apartment in Latsch.

The Fuchs family acquired Annenberg Castle in 2010 and has been producing wine in the region ever since.

until they acquired two more, very special properties, which brought with them a new hobby as well: wine-growing. In the small idyllic village of Altenburg, Caldaro, they bought an old manor house from the famous hiking guidebook writer Hanspaul Menara and extensively renovated it. The historic property had formerly been a "prison, local authority offices and public house, of which the famous German actor Heinz Rühmann had been a regular," reported Romana. It was bought with the intention to retire there, and was large enough to accommodate the whole family.

"He loved style and glamour!"

Adjoining the house is a small 6,000 m² vineyard where the grape varieties Pinot Blanc and Trollinger are grown. While the vineyard in Altenburg was long-established, the vines had to be newly planted at Annenberg Castle. This property towers over Latsch at around 1,000 m above sea level. As a child, Manfred is said to have dreamed of one day owning this castle, of which he had a full view from his parents' house. He was drawn to castles and to prestige his whole life. "He loved style and glamour!" said Romana. "Manfred always wanted nice things. Whenever something special came up for sale in South Tyrol, he wanted to know and then do a nice job of renovating it," said his friend Sepp. In 2009, the opportunity arose to put in an offer on Annenberg Castle. To acquire it and develop the former cattle farm into Annenberg Castle Vineyard, Manfred and Christa had to outbid some famous potential buyers including mountaineer Reinhold Messner and patron of the arts Walter Rizzi. There were two hectares on which to grow vines. "No one imagined it was possible to grow grapes so high up," said Sepp but "that was Manfred all over. He had no idea what he was doing, he just did it." It is only possible to grow grapes at that altitude now because the climate has become milder. And because this is such a recent occurrence, the wine labels are not permitted to bear the official names of the grape varieties, so the Fuchs' wines are labelled Luna (Kerner), Debut (Solaris), Aura (Scheurebe), Mars (Pinot Noir) and Venus (Zweigelt). In its very first year of bottling in 2013, Debut was awarded third place in the Freiburg State Viticulture Institute's wine tasting event. "Then Manfred wanted the best bottles, the best labels, even the best corks. For him, everything always had to be top quality," said Romed, who takes care of the management of the estate today. The Fuchs family gave the award-winning wines as Christmas presents to their employees as a special token of appreciation.

In the chapel of Saint Ann attached to the estate, Christa and Manfred renewed their marriage vows once again on 29th April 2010 to celebrate their golden wedding anniversary. Among the many guests was their friend Cardinal William Joseph Levada, then Prefect of the Roman Catholic Congregation for the Doctrine of the Faith, presenting a message from the Pope at the time, Benedict XVI. It was through the then mayor of Capri, Saverio Valente that they knew high-ranking clergy in the Vatican, including Cardinal Pio Laghi. Manfred didn't have any reservations about going straight up to people, so he "got direct access to VIPs," said both Sepp and Romed.

While South Tyrol has deep Roman Catholic roots, Manfred was never particularly religious. Besides, Christa is Protestant, which almost caused a row at Romana's christening in Latsch church because the priest wanted the mother of the child to remain at the back of the church on account of her religion. It was thanks entirely to the calming influence of Manfred's

The Fuchs family has a residence in Altenburg, Caldaro (left).

The photo below shows the family in the cellar of Annenberg Castle sampling the wine from their own vineyard.

Manfred and Christa Fuchs
celebrated their golden wedding
anniversary in South Tyrol with
many guests.

mother Paula – who did not want to cause an uproar in the small town – that a furious Manfred did not snatch up his daughter and have her christened elsewhere. Suffice it to say, there was no repeat episode at Marco's christening: for his baptism Christa stood front and centre. Although Manfred Fuchs was South Tyrolean through and through, he had one love which was stronger: that of his family!

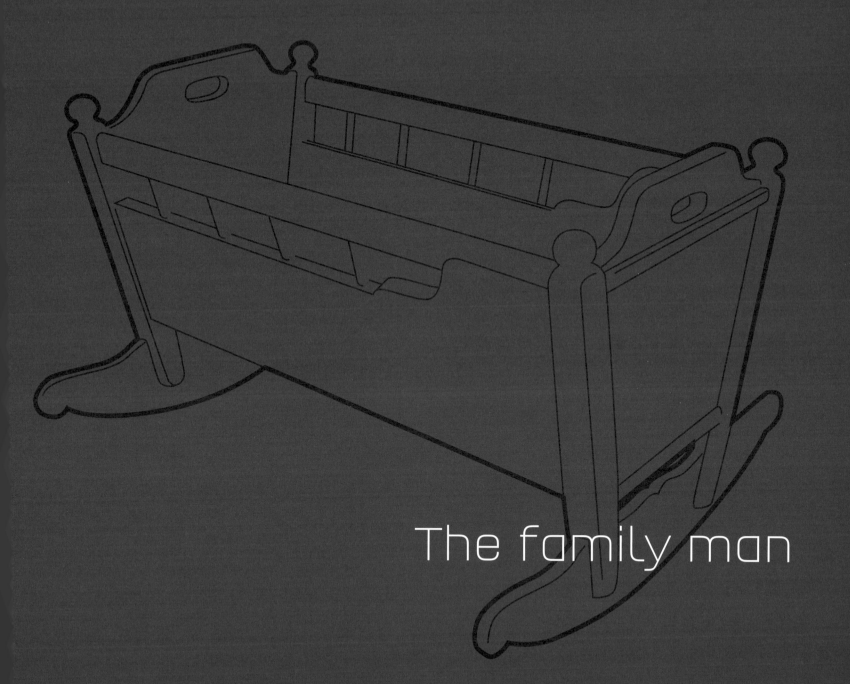

The family man

Living in the moment

He was a born entrepreneur, space enthusiast and visionary. Manfred Fuchs left home at the tender age of just 13 to pursue his chosen career. Despite this ambition, his business associates, friends and family say that he always had strong family values. So how did he manage to reconcile this with the busy schedule of a senior manager and later business owner?

No fewer than three of the ten members of his immediate family worked successfully side-by-side on a day-to-day basis in the family firm OHB. Marco's wife Christine also worked for OHB System for many years as a member of the Supervisory Board. To this day, Romana is Vice Chair of the Supervisory Board and, since as far back as 1993, has been contracted to provide legal services for the company on matters of patent and trademark law as well as during acquisition negotiations. She also manages the Fuchs family's real estate companies. Quite apart from the business side of things, Manfred's secret was the quality of the private time spent with his family and his ability to prioritise. When he was with his family, he was fully pres-

ent. He had the knack of living entirely in the moment. "When he took holidays, he left work behind," said Romed, remarking that his brother barely mentioned work at all when he was in South Tyrol. Even when a grandchild interrupted a meeting at OHB, he calmly listened to the child's chatter and all the managers and directors in the room – quite often a little put out – simply had to wait. However, his family values were in evidence long before this. Despite having left home so young, Manfred always kept in close contact with his South Tyrolean clan, as testified by his correspondence with his mother and sister as well as frequent visits home. "We didn't see much of each other because he left home so young, but whenever he came to visit, we always got on well," said Romed. Manfred spoke on the phone with his parents almost every week. His sister Inge married an Italian general and therefore moved around a lot. When she retired, she returned to Latsch and the three siblings' relationship was soured by property disputes. Manfred kept trying to settle their differences until the end. Again and again, he approached her in an effort to come to a resolution, but in vain. The situation really preyed on his mind, said his children. He wanted harmony in the family. Romana even described her father as non-confrontational in his private life. "He avoided conflict rather than seeking it out. He tended to dislike heated debate about family matters. 'It's all good, end of discussion, we're all agreed,' was his attitude." Her husband Peter agreed, adding, "Manfred didn't like to get bogged down in the details." Marco, too, described his relationship with his father as trouble-free: "I can't recall there ever being a time when I really clashed with my father, which is actually unusual."

The reason was probably that Manfred only ever looked in one direction: forward. It was not in his nature to dwell on the past. He is also described as not bearing

Manfred was born in the house by the sawmill operated by his grandfather Josef Fuchs and spent his early years there.

a grudge. "He gave it to you straight if he didn't like something, and that was it," said Romana.

"He avoided conflict rather than seeking it out."

Manfred's wife Christa described him, "like all the Fuchses", as a good father. Their parenting style was equitable and rather easy-going. "They never treated me and my brother differently. They never said anything like 'an education in home economics is good enough for you.' In that respect, my father was quite avant-garde for the time and his South Tyrolean roots," said Romana. There were certain ground rules and boundaries like "no stealing, no lying and keep your promises," but otherwise "neither of us was the sort of parent who put all that much thought into it. Of course, we wanted the children to be happy and healthy and to learn, but those were the guiding principles. We didn't need any sort of system," said Christa. Romana and Marco also described how the values were instilled in them by example rather than drilled into them. "When you grow up in an optimistic household, you simply don't have certain concerns. This fundamental confidence my father always had gave me a solid foundation. For one, it meant I had fewer anxieties," said Marco. One such value that Romana learned was "sticking together as a family, getting on, supporting and keeping in contact with one another." Another was the immense hospitality and generosity. Manfred's children and grandchildren mentioned these values in particular. Manfred and Christa insisted on paying when they ate out, and always tipped generously. Their financial input went much further than that, however. Both believed in giving something back to society, both

Manfred with his godfather Mr Peccolo.

Manfred with his sister Inge in Munich, as a new father with his newborn daughter Romana in Hamburg and relaxing in the garden in South Tyrol with Marco and Romana.

in South Tyrol and in Germany. For example, they supported the arts and charitable causes as well as conventional aerospace activities and institutions.

Quite apart from his open-handedness, Manfred was said to be generous with immaterial things as well. One could call it tolerance. The interesting thing is that he was also considered the undisputed head of the family, a patriarch; the "quintessential Fuchs", as Marco's son Konstantin put it. Though he was very quiet, very relaxed and had the patience of a saint, he had very clear ideas and preferences as to how things should be. His ability to carry off these two characteristics was due, for one, to his "natural authority and charisma. When he came into the room, he had presence. He had great powers of persuasion and self-confidence and was able to convince people of his ideas," said Romana. Marco, too, mentioned that his father was not a great believer in collective decisions. "He always thought that the world works better when there are clear directions," said Marco. Despite that, Manfred did not leave an authoritarian impression on his family. "He was always open to and interested in other opinions and ideas when they made sense to him," said Christine Fuchs. He could even "anticipate other people's interest," was how Marco put it. It seems almost commonplace, but this ability is critical for respectful interactions between people and also for getting ahead in business. "He was a good listener and always understood that the environment has its own agenda and one had to take care to adapt to it and to put all participants at ease," said Marco, who attributed Manfred's capacity to do so to the village community from which he hailed. In contrast to the anonymity of a big city, people paid much closer attention to one another there.

Unlike parties with friends, where Manfred was always the entertainer, at family get-togethers, Manfred tended to "withdraw into the hustle and bustle", said Christine of her father-in-law. Of course, with ten in the immediate family, sometimes things used to get rowdy. When the meal was ready or Manfred wanted to be heard, he gave a loud piercing whistle that went right through you. Manfred was used to large families. In the early years, he himself lived with his grand-parents, uncles, aunts and twelve cousins at the saw-mill. Manfred would have liked three or more children but Christa didn't want any more after Romana and Marco because she actually wanted to return to work as well, but "back then, he wanted a career, so I had to stay at home." However, once the children were in school, she got herself a job. "She wasn't a housewife by choice, more out of necessity. It was never what she truly wanted. It simply wasn't enough for her. She started working again relatively quickly, at Café Jacobs on Saturdays," said Romana. Her mother was a "housewife out of necessity" because Manfred often travelled abroad even early in his career. He wasn't away just for the day, but weeks even and sometimes months at a time on business trips or for the rocket launches in Australia. As was common at the time, his family rarely saw him but "when my father was there, he was fully present and did a lot with us, made things with us, told us South Tyrolean legends and took us on outings. At children's parties, he was always the hero with his stories and games," recalled Romana, adding, "We didn't see a lot of him, which was why we had such great times in South Tyrol, where we were always together for a good long time."

Manfred and Christa as a young couple. She was a housewife "out of necessity" and sought work as soon as the opportunity arose.

Visiting Grandma Paula: Marco, Christa and Romana on one of their holidays in South Tyrol.

Grandchildren David, Gabriel, Konstantin, Blanca and Raphaela in Gran Canaria, one of the Fuchs family's favourite holiday destinations. Romana in Sioux City Park, trying her hand at rodeo riding.

"He was a good granddad. He was always good to everyone and it was so sweet the way he used to carry Grandma's handbag."

Unlike other managers or business owners, Manfred had always taken time for family holidays. He was even the driving force when it came to organising regular get-togethers and bringing the clan together. In addition to the family's visits to South Tyrol and the traditional get-togethers on all the major holidays, he later initiated a family holiday in Gran Canaria. The family used to spend time together on the Canary Island every autumn "to extend the summer". The children and grandchildren went paintballing, go-karting and swimming in the Sioux City Wild West theme park, while Manfred and Christa took it easy. Sure, he liked the Wild West park too, but otherwise he enjoyed the fine weather, the peace and quiet and reading the paper meticulously from front to back: one of his favourite pastimes his whole life long. Privately, Manfred's interests were very diverse as well and he could immerse himself completely in an interesting article he came across in the newspaper or a programme on the television. Once, Marco was surprised to find him watching cycling, completely enthralled. "Since when are you interested in cycling?" he asked and was taken aback by the answer. "Since always. I used to love watching the Giro d'Italia as a boy!" This capacity for genuine interest in various subjects and people and ability to live entirely in the moment was also an important stress-buster. Apart from the fact

Romed and Jolanda on a visit to Hamburg.

Manfred was very resourceful privately as well and his self-penned musical performances were always entertaining at parties.

Manfred with his grand-
daughter Blanca in his arms.

that Manfred was hardly ever stressed because of the way he was and his disposition, living in the moment enabled him to recharge his batteries. "He lay down and fell asleep straight away," said both Christa and Christine. "He was very good at switching off. He was able to say, 'I have such-and-such a function on and no matter how I feel or how tired I am, I'm going. Or he'd say, 'Now I'm having a rest.'" And the world could fall down around him. Even in the tough times – for instance, when OHB was in crisis – his family never got the feeling that there was cause for worry. "My father's experience was that things worked out well in life. He never really suffered losses or setbacks. He never had internal struggles, self-doubt or uncertainty. His fundamental attitude was 'I am good at what I do, so everything is just fine,'" said Marco, who also had the feeling that his father strove to ensure that his side of the family in South Tyrol gained financial prestige because Manfred's parents were not as well off as Romedius' ancestors and some of his siblings. Konstantin always had the feeling "that Manfred wanted to build a dynasty. He wanted to offer his family – his children – something." He certainly achieved that financially and even surpassed his own hopes.

Far nicer than that, however, are the recollections of his grandchildren, who were his pride and joy, because the personal moments and experiences left a deeper impression on their memories than Manfred's professional achievements. Romana's son Gabriel, for example, remembers that Manfred taught him to tell the time in the swimming pool in Gran Canaria. Konstantin is also reminded of his grandfather when he squirts water out of his hand in the pool because Manfred showed him how to do that in the open-air pool in Huchting. Romana's daughter Raphaela said, "He was a good granddad. He was always good to everyone and it was so sweet the way he used to carry Grandma's

Granddad Manfred with his first grandchild, Romana's son David, in his arms.

Romana Fuchs Mayrhofer and
her husband Peter at one of
the Fuchs family parties.

Manfred's grandchildren
(left to right) Blanca,
Raphaela, Gabriel and
Konstantin climbing near
Altenburg in South Tyrol.

handbag." Such seeming trivialities are lasting images in the grandchildren's minds when they think of their granddad. They also show that he had a lot of time for them. All five agree that he was always calm and collected, cheerful, friendly and extremely relaxed. Manfred didn't talk about work in front of them, nor did he try to steer them towards a technical education. On the contrary, as with his own children, he gave them freedom to develop and encouraged them to find their own way. "You have to do what pleases you most. Even if something embarrassing happens, no harm done." "Make a fool of yourself once a day" was one of his sayings and an enduring memory of David, Romana's eldest son.

He, like his sister Raphaela, recalls that Manfred "was always nice to all people", no matter their background. This trait inspired their shared life's motto: "Always treat people as you want to be treated." Marco's daughter Blanca, too, learned from her grandfather that "no matter how high you soar, stay grounded." Plus she shares his curiosity about the world. "He was very well travelled, tried so many things and never stopped exploring the world." Manfred constantly inspired the family with his undiminished optimism. His son-in-law Peter greatly enjoyed "the many fascinating conversations with Manfred at the chalet. He always gave me courage to take on new challenges."

That was how Manfred lived his life too, "as intended and imagined, and that really is enviable," thought Christine and Blanca. Gabriel, too, holds up his grandfather's life as an example: "He did what he wanted. He had big dreams, stayed true to them and made them reality." Romana takes Manfred as an example "because he always did what he said. He was a man of his word. He was authentic, you could rely on him." Manfred was no different in his professional life.

A dream team both privately and professionally: Christa and Manfred Fuchs.

David, boating with his granddad in Bürgerpark Bremen.

His legacy goes far beyond a respected, successful space enterprise. He inspired his children and grand-children and gave them the freedom to develop. They still meet with their South Tyrolean relations for cabin parties and other occasions, share fond memories of Manfred and bring both his material legacy and ideals out into the world; a world about which Manfred was so very curious, right up to the end of his days.

Romana and the proud grandparents with David.

Marco's daughter Blanca holding on tight to Dad and Granddad.

"He did what he wanted.
He had big dreams,
stayed true to them and
made them reality."

Manfred visibly feels at ease
among his children and
grandchildren.

Traditional Christmas brunch with the family in Bremen: Christine's parents Rüdiger and Margit Klein, Konstantin, Christa, Marco, Blanca and Christine.

The entrepreneur

Courage to take the leap

There is a long history of enterprise in Manfred Fuchs' family. Here we see, from left to right: a waiter, Manfred's grandfather Josef Fuchs in front of his guesthouse "Ebner" in Absam near Innbruck, Meinrad Stricker with his wife Leni (née Fuchs), Martin, "Nana" Anna Gamper and Rudel Fuchs.

Manfred Fuchs was quite literally born into entrepreneurship. Almost all his relations in South Tyrol worked in businesses they owned and many still do to this very day. Even in the ERNO days, Manfred longed to run his own business one day as well. His original idea was a hotel in South Tyrol. He often spoke of this plan and gave credence to it by buying property in the region. Then the opportunity arose to take over the small business OHB. He seized it, and his wish to become an entrepreneur became reality in the mid-1980s. Of course, it is important to acknowledge that OHB is a family operation, and Christa and Marco Fuchs' achievements also deserve credit for the success of the

business. However, that in itself is an important personality trait of a good entrepreneur: he must be able to choose the right partners to help him build, run and grow the business.

At any rate, Manfred Fuchs possessed pretty much all the characteristics which, economic theory holds, make a successful entrepreneur. His foresight and willingness to take risks have already been mentioned numerous times. Taking the leap from ERNO to OHB also demonstrated these qualities. He had put years of preparation into the move, even though it was essentially Plan B. When his wife initially took over OHB, it

Manfred Fuchs had all the
characteristics that make a
successful entrepreneur.

was not certain whether Manfred Fuchs would later join the business himself or take more of a back seat. What is certain is that the merger of ERNO and MBB did not serve him well. He risked losing face if he stayed. He was proactive and devised an exit strategy in the form of OHB if the worst came to the worst, which it did in 1985. Manfred Fuchs was passed over for the role of head of the whole of Sales, a position he deserved, and it was only then – arguably in protest, but of his own volition – that he left MBB/ERNO overnight. He had

foreseen this eventuality as far back as the beginning of the 1980s, but he remained loyal to his employer in his final five years at the company. During this time, he did his job and drove on projects and supported the debate about the project leadership of Columbus with the same vigour with which he lobbied for satellites to continue to be developed and built in Bremen. Gerhard Schneider, then responsible for the ERNO satellite division, recalled this time: "Although we had been informed that all satellite activities would move south

The ERNO building at Hünefeldstrasse 1–5 was Manfred Fuchs' place of work until 1985. He left to become self-employed at OHB.

The securing of the project leadership for the telecommunications satellite DFS Kopernikus was thanks in part to Manfred Fuchs' efforts at MBB/ERNO in Bremen.

after the merger, we still ended up building Koperni-kus and also had a good deal of input on Hipparcos and Meteosat. We successfully made a stand against the decision. Without doubt, Manfred was the one in the wings giving me strength." At the same time, he also saw to it that his wife's company was able to grow. Ini-tially, they took on whatever work they could get to keep the firm afloat and earn money: this is another quality that defines the successful entrepreneur.

Their order book in the first few years ranged from their original line of work for the armed forces to fitting out containers for testing stations on Heligoland, overhauling heavy-load carriers, a label reading

"In difficult situations, one could always be certain of his empathy and willingness to help."

machine and a hand skimmer all the way up to pollu-tion control vessels, which had already been in the pipeline in an alliance with MBB/ERNO and the Sarstedt shipyard. Of course, the grand objective – especially after Manfred Fuchs transferred to OHB – was to build up an engineering firm with a strong emphasis on

One of OHB's early projects was the optoelectronic monitor "Elba 1", which could read labels on bottles and glasses.

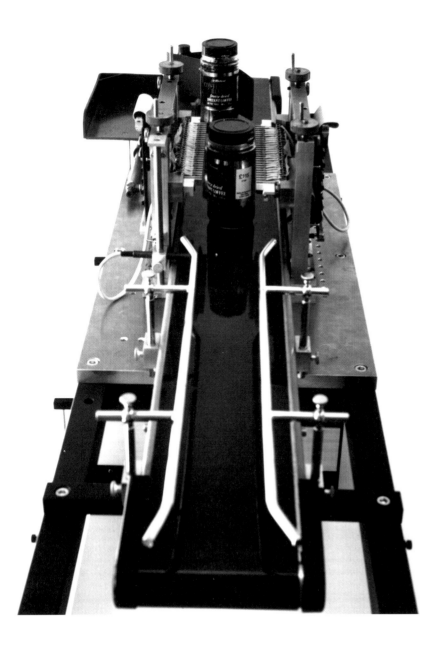

space flight. That was the vision that inspired him and drove him. However, to make it reality, neither he nor his employees were ever above literally rolling up their sleeves and working nights and weekends on all sorts of contracts. That even meant crawling through ships to get to grips with the task at hand and taking home test setups so they could run 24/7 without the risk of being accidentally unplugged by a co-worker. In the early years of being self-employed, Manfred Fuchs had to start from scratch and be willing to take risks; enter into consulting contracts with other firms in the space industry and, of course, by all means possible find a niche for small and medium enterprises, which OHB once was. He realised that the space industry was moving out of his reach and, in order to get in on the space agenda, he needed to offer an alternative to the big players. He put great energy into promoting SMEs in the industry. It was his efforts that led to the introduction of a rule that the commissioning agencies had to award a certain proportion of the contract value to SMEs. This applied to Germany initially, and later throughout Europe, for ESA contracts, when Manfred Fuchs helped to initiate the SME Space Alliance to protect "the minnows". He occasionally chaired DLR and ESA meetings and debated the prevailing status in the SME space sector in Germany. He presented ideas for new technological developments and gained associates and advocates for his projects. Of course, Manfred Fuchs' perspective was coloured by OHB's interests, but it must also be said that he always acted very much in the interests of progressing space flight. Given a conflict of interests between the industry partners involved, he sought consensus and did so with such diplomacy and finesse that the parties generally came to an agreement. Director General of the ESA, Prof. Dr Jan Wörner, put it in a nutshell in his obituary of Manfred Fuchs: "The more I got to know him, the more I saw his qualities outside of the world of work, and it was those

Felix Anchuelo at work: OHB serviced charging devices, among other things, for its client, the German armed forces.

Associates and advocates (left to right): Dr Fritz Merkle, astronaut Thomas Reiter and the then chairman of the executive board of the DLR, Johann-Dietrich "Jan" Wörner, with Manfred Fuchs at OHB.

In the early years, OHB overhauled heavy-load carriers, such as "Kamag" and "Scheuerle".

They could transport components weighing between 65 and 450 tonnes.

qualities which always impressed me the most. He was quick to gauge the mood – positive or negative – and did everything he could, including engaging at a personal level, to get the chemistry right. And he succeeded. Rank and hierarchy were immaterial. In difficult situations, you could always rely on his empathy and willingness to help."

He was, simply, the perfect team player. His great charisma is unforgettable. He made full use of it to build up a rock-solid network of like-minded people and, with that, to create anchor points in business and, above all, in the world of politics, to feed these movers and shakers with information about policy relating to space flight and to get them on board with his visions and the projects he wanted to pursue. Manfred Fuchs was a master at it. He was also a remarkable judge of human nature, which enabled him to find and utilise the right people for his ideas, visions and projects. Some of his associates describe the personal relationships that evolved with Manfred Fuchs as very special, indeed sometimes as very close and cordial. Manfred Fuchs was always very considerate of others. He made sure that interactions were fair and solution-oriented, with give-and-take on both sides. Among clients he was regarded as open, honest and, above all, reliable. When he made promises, one could be certain that he would do everything in his power to keep them. All of these were additional strengths that make a successful entrepreneur.

Often his promises to the client were very accommodating technically or in terms of timing. But his employees went along with him. As far back as the Predevelopment days at ERNO, Manfred Fuchs was able to create a very productive working environment, mainly because he was loyal to his team, did not let them down and did not embarrass anyone if something did go awry. He gave his people every liberty as long as they delivered results. So, it's not surprising that Manfred Fuchs' team would have done anything for him, as Gerhard Schneider stated. He brought this laissez-faire attitude with him to OHB. Many employees have reported that they could do pretty much anything they pleased, especially in the early days. Complete freedom was afforded to innovative thinking and approaches, the only condition being that something had to come of it. Of course, the flip side was that employees had to work hard. They had to be cut out for it. However, most were up for it because they believed in this one man and his start-up and they threw all caution to the wind to embark on the OHB adventure. Manfred Fuchs' charisma and promises were enough for them to believe in the space company dream. This very same charisma and his convincing depictions of the future enabled him to gather around him people, almost all of whom were lone operators but who were totally committed to him.

The then Director General of the ESA, Jean-Jacques Dordain, with Manfred Fuchs. He was considered a reliable client and fair project partner.

View of the interior of the
Biolab. After initial problems,
OHB brought the project to a
very successful conclusion.

In addition, another factor in his success as an entrepreneur was his spontaneity and decisiveness. They
gave him and OHB the flexibility to act and react quickly. For example, when, in 1995, the company needed help
on the Biolab life-support system because the project
was on the verge of failure, Dr Rüdiger Schönfeld, today
head of MTG projects, was invited to come from Brun-
swick for an interview. The two men met on a Thursday.
Once they shook on it, Manfred Fuchs said, "You start
on Monday. Sure, you have the whole weekend to move."
And that's the way it happened. Because Manfred was
a good judge of character, he had found the right man
for the challenge, plus he had shown clear thinking in a
crisis and in the end handed over to the client a
life-support system with excellent functionality on
favourable terms, as promised.

Team players at work (from
near left): Dr Fritz Merkle,
Hans Hoffmann, Gerhard
Schneider, Marco, Christa
and Manfred Fuchs, Wolfgang
Wienss, Herbert Ludwig,
Peter Natenbruck and
Dr Detlev Hüser.

The tradition continues: even after Manfred Fuchs' death, the lavish parties still take place.
This picture was taken at Christmas 2014 in Hotel zur Munte in Bremen.

On the one hand, Manfred Fuchs demanded no small amount of his employees, but, on the other, he was also very approachable and empathetic. He had a genuine interest in those around him, which many a time went beyond the professional. If employees got into difficulty in their personal lives, he helped where he could. He was loyal and, like at ERNO, didn't let people down. There were no terminations. This created stability and led to a willingness on the part of his team to work that bit harder to meet tight deadlines or go that extra mile for the firm.

He himself liked to do his rounds of the firm every morning, greeting all the staff in person and exchang-

ing a few words with them. Of course, as time went on and the number of employees grew, this changed. Then he met them at events such as summer parties, birthday and Christmas parties. He was always a jocular and generous host. On very hot summer days he used to bring in ice cream to cool everyone down. He saw the staff almost as family. For a long time, the relationship between employer and employee was of mutual trust and his staff even tolerated the pay freezes that were required after the ABRIXAS failure. When imposing the pay freeze, Manfred Fuchs promised to make up for it once they won the SAR-Lupe contract. He kept his promise.

The EPIRB maritime search and rescue beacon was one of OHB's first products.

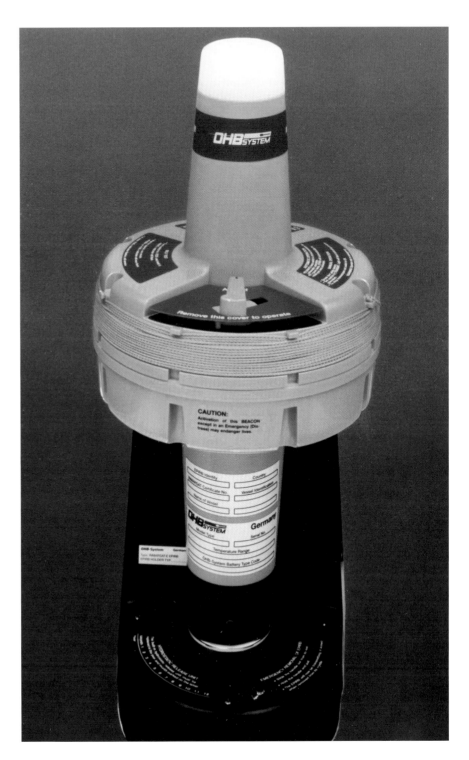

Thus, one step at a time, he and his team made progress. He was always well-prepared with his enterprising persistence and perseverance. He set himself short-, medium- and long-term goals, then carefully worked through them and didn't lose sight of his eventual target. For example, in the early days, OHB's main activity, marine technology and the pollution control vessels, was expanded to include maritime search and rescue beacons. This led him to adopt the mission statement "sea to sky". The idea for a maritime alert and guidance system was conceived and the beacons – referred to as EPIRBs – were linked to the ground stations via the Inmarsat satellite system. He presented this concept at numerous trade fairs and to the space agencies – with success.

As it was, Manfred Fuchs was tirelessly marketing whatever products his fledgling firm had to offer while planning his next moves into space flight. While, at that time, some of the other companies in the industry were developing very complex space flight components, he tried to do the opposite, using simple but effective means. He was not afraid to buy in standard parts and qualify them for use in space. He constantly put forward the argument that space technology did not necessarily have to be expensive and proved it with his practicable solutions. At any rate, pricing was one of his resounding successes in what was otherwise a very costly industry. For instance, he thought of numerous less expensive alternatives to zero-gravity experiments in outer space – such as drop capsules and parabolic flight – and expanded the scope for scientific users. Later, he reduced the microgravity times required for experiments, which led to a further drop in costs after the completion of the Bremen drop tower. From 1975, he pushed for its construction in the national and local committees and saw to it that the plans were implemented.

126

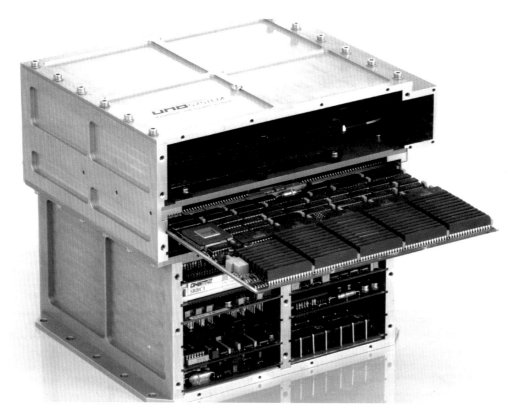

SAFIR's "brain" was the on-board computer and, after BremSat, ushered OHB into the satellite systems business.

These strategies – initially developed and planned by him alone – led to his firm's entry into space flight. Not only that, but one of his chief ambitions in business was to establish engineering services at OHB, with the result that the agitation tank, the first component suitable for use in space, was developed, qualified and built there. The OHB engineers successfully worked their way up to major contracts for the European Columbus module for the ISS via an electronics box for recording and controlling microgravity experiments, Cosima, contributions to the D1 and D2 missions and to MIR, a great many biological experiments and the Anthrorack. All this time, Manfred Fuchs was realising his pioneering visions through the use of small satellites, which gave him and OHB their break. He showed he had the necessary stamina and determination in this endeavour too, going from a role in a small scientific satellite all the way up to supplying entire systems for reconnaissance, Earth observation, navigation, weather and communications satellites. He did not build the first free-flying proprietary OHB satellite until he had done a trial run with ZARM and his engineers based on BremSat. After the project proved successful, SAFIR was next. SAFIR marked OHB's entry into the systems satellite business, which would dominate its ventures from then on.

Alexander Gerst took this
shot from the ISS in 2014.
Manfred Fuchs and OHB
played a major part in the
development of the space
station.

However, OHB's growth was not confined to the number of projects and the expansion of its range of services. An important step for the business was the Fuchs family's decision to go to IPO, the only German space company to do so. From the outset, the family held two thirds of the shares and therefore retained control.

"My father got his gambling streak from his South Tyrolean side. He came from a world where enterprise can be ad hoc."

Following the IPO in 2002, which was spearheaded by Marco Fuchs, the three Fuchses made for a successful team with their respective strengths in business. While Manfred continued as before as head of the technical side, his son Marco became responsible for the growth strategy through acquisitions. Within the triad, Christa Fuchs always occupied the role of financial regulator. However, her sphere of influence was much broader than that: although her husband often took decisions about projects unilaterally and even made the following note in one of his journals, "The lone eagle flies higher", he did discuss them with his wife, who sometimes managed to change his mind when she had concerns or considered it too risky for OHB. For example, she was vehemently against the takeover of the three Airbus plants, Varel, Nordenham and Augsburg in 2007. Nor did she agree with a proposal for reconnaissance satellites for Turkey. Manfred Fuchs went ahead anyway and lost. His spontaneity was, without doubt, part of his success. However, sometimes his quick thinking

Executives Ulrich Schulz,
Marco and Manfred Fuchs
are pleased about the IPO.

and impulsive enthusiasm found another outlet, especially in private. "My father liked to gamble. If we were
ever in a casino, he was always the last to leave and the
one who spent the most. He enjoyed it. It was the same
with investments. My mother put a stop to lots of ventures which would have been a complete flop," said
Marco Fuchs, describing his father's gambling predi-
lection and citing investments he had planned, especially in hotels in East Germany, South Tyrol and Saudi
Arabia – some of which were totally run down. When
Manfred Fuchs was all fired up about something, his
wife and son would often wait in silence to see whether
his euphoria abated by itself; if not, they would inter-
vene together. "My father got his gambling streak from
his South Tyrolean side. He came from a world where
enterprise can be ad hoc," said Marco Fuchs.

The working relationship
with the Russian project
partners was often ad hoc
and uncomplicated, a
mentality that defined the
entrepreneur Manfred Fuchs.

An unbeatable trio: OHB's
success comes down to the
achievements of Marco,
Christa and Manfred Fuchs.

Spirits were high at OHB during a visit from the D2 crew: Manfred Fuchs literally and figuratively prostrated himself before clients and employees.

Business strategy at OHB was also a matter for the family right to the end. The decision-making paths were short: the offices were always side by side. Without doubt, OHB would not be the company it is today but for the family's entrepreneurial spirit. That said, it was clearly Manfred Fuchs who laid the solid foundation. With amazing foresight, continuity and entrepreneurial ability he transformed a small work-shop into a space company and left it with good prospects for the future as well as handing over the reins to the next generation. He managed to make the leap from SME to a big player, a systems firm, and lived to see OHB's subsequent successes.

The entrepreneur Manfred Fuchs, without doubt, played a large part in advancing space activities in Germany and Europe, in ensuring that Bremen is a centre of space flight today and that OHB is a space concern with activities all across Europe and one of the top three in the industry. However, as a company boss, his exceptional personal qualities above all, his forth-rightness and his reliability were what set him apart.

Spaceman extraordinaire

Living for space flight

cialised area as well as to make his own mark quickly must have tempted Manfred. He always wanted to be outstanding in his field; but that is only possible when one has a passion for one's job and a grasp of the subject area and the bigger picture. Manfred certainly had that. He rigorously pursued his goal, starting with his attendance of technical school. He picked up the requisite space expertise as he went along. He was masterful at strategy, setting the right priorities and winning over the people around him.

The South Tyrolean Manfred Fuchs began his technical education in Bolzano at the young age of 13.

As long ago as the beginning of the 20th century, the Tyrolean Max Valier worked on rocket engines, with which he intended to conquer space. Manfred Fuchs was fascinated by his compatriot.

Once there was a little boy who loved technology and dreamed of flying. Even before he left his home town of Latsch, the young Manfred had heard of Max Valier (*1895, †1930), a fellow South Tyrolean from Bolzano who had made his mark with the development of rocket engines. He conducted audacious experiments in preparation for the construction of rocket ships he intended to fire into space. However, a failed test cost him his life at a young age. At the same time, thrilling stories were going round about Hermann Oberth and others on the subject of expeditions to the Moon. In Latsch and later in Bolzano, Munich and Hamburg, the focus of Manfred Fuchs' fascination and studies was initially the fundamentals of aviation. However, when the northern development consortium (Entwicklungsring Nord – ERNO) was established, he jumped at the chance to play an active role in the development of the space industry in Germany and Europe even though he was more or less self-taught. The opportunity to try his hand in a new branch of industry, to grow into this spe-

His time at ERNO in Bremen opened up every door to the various different applications of space flight. First, he himself worked hands-on on the development of the third stage of the proposed EUROPA rocket. However, he was quick to see the bigger picture and gave his Predevelopment engineers carte blanche to exploit the full range of possibilities: from launch vehicles to space laboratories and weightlessness experiments and on to re-entry vehicles and satellites. The powers that had shaped the space agenda until the 1970s had been motivated by prestige, but it dawned on them that space technology could greatly improve and increase the benefit of many areas of communication, weather forecasting and Earth observation.

However, the economic aspect is only half the story. Ultimately, space flight is first and foremost about curiosity and risk-taking. Manfred Fuchs had the "imagination and dynamism" stemming from his South Tyrolean background, as his friend Prof. Ernesto Vallerani put it. Coupled with his German efficiency and sincerity, Manfred therefore represented the perfect combination of both nationalities, making him the ideal candidate to push ahead with the space effort. Firstly, one must cast off the conventions of the Earth to find new technologies and advancements and to venture into distant, unfamiliar territories. Secondly, the ideas must be physically and financially possible. Manfred Fuchs always had a special talent for feasibility and never strayed into the realm of the impracticable. His vision of space flight was to advance humankind, obtain findings for research and science, broaden the horizons and yet still also remain cost-effective. He was able to develop demand and strategies. Once the goals were set, in order to obtain funding, they had to be put into terms that politicians could understand. Manfred was a master of that as well. Not only was he able to present the subject matter convincingly, but he had a knack of winning over and filling people with enthusiasm. There are a number of examples of this, which also illustrate his creative powers, his foresight and his influence on space flight in Europe, and Germany in particular. Some of them are important milestones in the history of European space flight.

Manfred Fuchs grew up with the inspiring works of the pioneer of rocketry Hermann Oberth, who wrote "The Rocket into Planetary Space" as far back as 1923 and published his book "Ways to Spaceflight" in 1929.

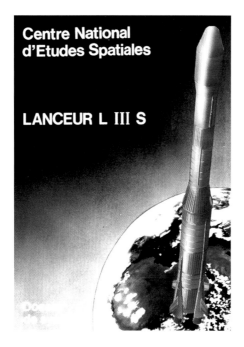

The design of the third-generation substitution launcher (Lanceur 3ème Génération Substitution) marked a turning point away from the Europa rocket towards the ARIANE.

Manfred Fuchs framed this picture of Hermann Oberth, Wernher von Braun and Dr Friedrich Staats and had it on display in his office.

SPACELAB AND ENTRY INTO MANNED SPACE FLIGHT

Despite Manfred Fuchs' department's comprehensive preparations, ERNO wasn't awarded a role in developing the Space Shuttle because the US military, the lead partner on the project, rejected the European proposal to participate in the programme. Manfred and his team then contemplated how the Shuttle could be used other than for transportation. One idea that hadn't yet been given due consideration in America was research in zero gravity. Astronauts should research living and working in space and thereby advance manned space flight. With that, the concept of Spacelab as the European contribution to the Americans' post-Apollo programme was born. The first studies to be done on this, in 1972, triggered a competition between the space companies in Europe for the contract. Manfred Fuchs blazed a trail here too. He and his team at ERNO developed a modular concept for the research laboratory. He then pitched this proposal to his Italian industry partners in particular as well as his most important political friends. They took up the cause and lobbied for it in the right circles, with the result that, in 1973, the ESA Ministerial Council gave the Spacelab programme under German leadership the green light. Thanks to its flexible and robust concept proposal, ERNO secured the contract to build the space laboratory. This cleared the way for Europe to participate in manned space flight. The role of Manfred Fuchs, Ernesto Vallerani and Gottfried Greger was significant, and they should be recognised as Europe's ushers into manned space flight, also because they were subsequently instrumental in driving forward the Columbus programme as the European contribution to the International Space Station ISS.

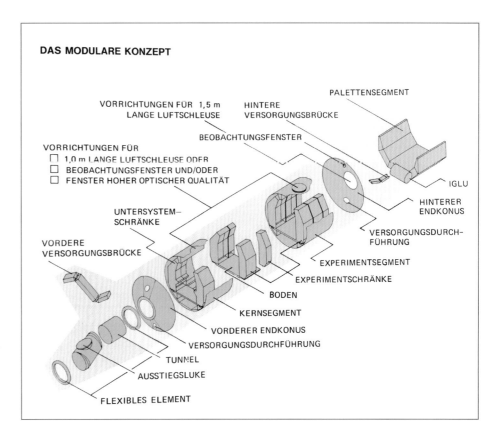

DAS MODULARE KONZEPT

VORRICHTUNGEN FÜR 1,5 m LANGE LUFTSCHLEUSE

HINTERE VERSORGUNGSBRÜCKE

PALETTENSEGMENT

BEOBACHTUNGSFENSTER

VORRICHTUNGEN FÜR
- 1,0 m LANGE LUFTSCHLEUSE ODER
- BEOBACHTUNGSFENSTER UND/ODER
- FENSTER HOHER OPTISCHER QUALITÄT

IGLU

HINTERER ENDKONUS

UNTERSYSTEM-SCHRÄNKE

VERSORGUNGSDURCH-FÜHRUNG

VORDERE VERSORGUNGSBRÜCKE

EXPERIMENTSEGMENT

EXPERIMENTSCHRÄNKE

BODEN

KERNSEGMENT

VORDERER ENDKONUS

VERSORGUNGSDURCHFÜHRUNG

TUNNEL

AUSSTIEGSLUKE

FLEXIBLES ELEMENT

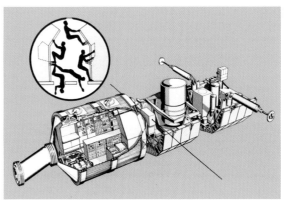

Versatile, fast turnaround, and low-cost operation: ERNO's modular concept for the Spacelab won the competition.

The space station was also a prospect: the illustration shows how NASA imagined the station in 1976.

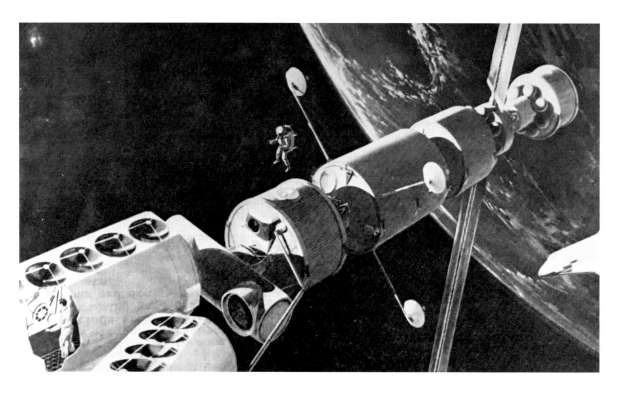

Just one year later, ERNO built the Space Sled (right) for medical research on the first Spacelab mission.

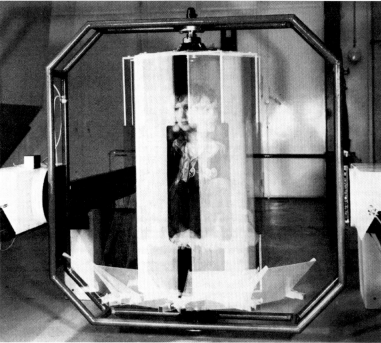

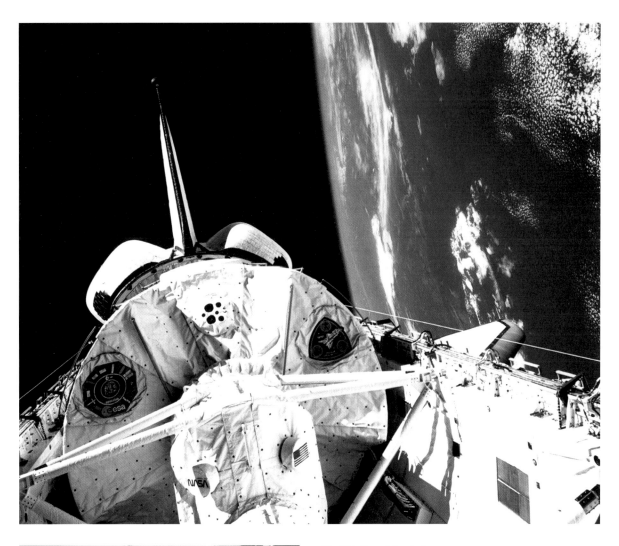

The fifth Spacelab mission was carried by the Shuttle Columbia in 1991 (top).

On the D2 mission two years later, the German astronaut Hans Wilhelm Schlegel was on board the Space Shuttle Atlantis.

The MIKROBA drop capsule provided a low-cost alternative for preparing microgravity experiments for space missions.

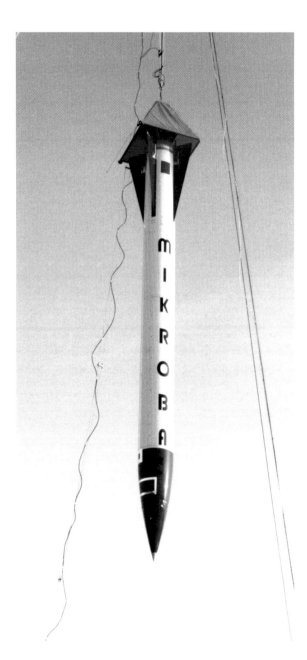

MICROGRAVITY RESEARCH AND THE SPACE STATION

After the success of Spacelab, Manfred Fuchs not only worked on the programme itself but also focused on the definition, development and construction of experiments for the space laboratory. It was clear to him that he had to arouse the interests of scientists and potential users quickly. With the support of those at the helm in politics and in the space industry, the Spacelab utilisation working group ASN was set up and he later became its Chairman. He wanted to be able to deliver research results in the future in order to gain acceptance for "his" space laboratory, especially as opposition was mounting from scientists who were vehemently against manned space flight because they regarded robotic missions as safer and less costly. Therefore, Manfred was hoping for Spacelab to deliver satisfactory results, in particular the national D1 and D2 missions and from the Russian space station MIR, to garner acceptance for manned missions. He also made sure there was public debate about the possibilities of Spacelab. For him, space flight was not something to be kept secret, but should be explained to the person on the street, who, ultimately, bore some of the substantial costs and had a right to transparency. Manfred knew that the expensive space experiments had to be well prepared. He therefore sought and found ways to test and improve them for their missions in space using parabolic flights, drop capsules and rocket programmes. He advanced this affordable version of microgravity experiments his whole life. At OHB, too, he began with parabolic flights and drop capsules before moving on to larger projects. OHB also worked on re-entry technologies, such as TOPAS, Raumkurier, EXPRESS and FALKE. Later, the firm built racks for the Columbus space laboratory and developed some experiments for the space station,

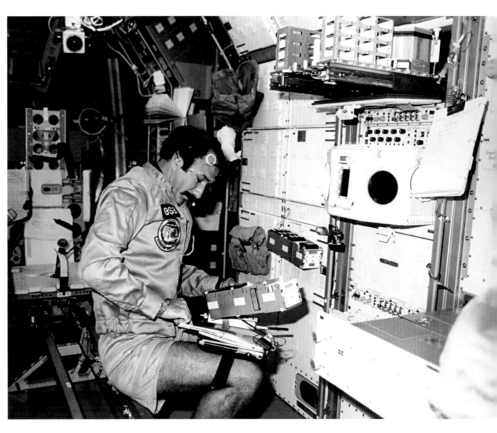

including experiments in the fields of materials science, medicine and biology. For example, the South American clawed frog nicknamed Manni once flew into space as a tadpole in the space aquarium CEBAS and on his return lived for some years in the Life Sciences department of OHB as a much-revered "frogonaut". This programme strand recently culminated in the new firm "Blue Horizon", whose mission it is to develop and exploit space resources and help to make it possible to live on other planets. This goes to show how farsighted the spaceman extraordinaire Manfred Fuchs was: he always knew the importance of maintaining expertise in his firm, even when they were not generating any profits for the moment.

Manni the "frogonaut" in OHB's aquarium.

The Dutch astronaut Wubbo Ockels in the Spacelab on the D1 mission in 1985.

TEXUS experiments were fitted in the payload module at ERNO for mission launch from Kiruna in December 1977.

BREMEN, CENTRE OF SPACE FLIGHT

Space projects and the technologies required to execute them can only flourish in an environment in which they can adapt to a huge variety of demands according to the current requirements. Such an environment did not exist when space activities started up in Bremen. The model for Manfred Fuchs was MBB and Munich. There was a university to educate the next generation; there were research institutes to define the projects, to support and steward them; there were industrial firms to deliver the products for the projects. Spaceman extraordinaire Manfred Fuchs realised as long ago as 1975 that Bremen would develop into a centre for space flight in Europe thanks to Spacelab, the application and research satellites and ARIANE. While his prediction that "preparations for the exploitation of space should be completed in the early 1980s" was not entirely accurate, he did understand that he had to restructure Bremen for his vision of space flight, and strove to achieve this goal.

After OHB moved from Bremen-Hemelingen into the newly developed Technology Park in close proximity to the University of Bremen in 1988, Manfred Fuchs also began to prepare his environment for space flight. The Center of Applied Space Technology and Microgravity (ZARM) was founded at the University of Bremen. His first sketches of the Bremen drop tower hail from that same year. This was an idea he had been presenting to and debating in the ZARM interest group and in political circles. In fact, he began negotiations with the political authorities as far back as 1986. By 1990, construction of the drop tower was complete and it began operating soon after. The BremSat microsatellite was also built in collaboration with ZARM. In 1994, it was successfully launched into space on board the Shuttle. Spaceman extraordinaire Manfred Fuchs and his firm OHB both

benefited from this. He lit a beacon for Bremen as a centre of space flight and his support demonstrated that his engineers had achieved systems capability. Later, he initiated the BEOS development programme for the state of Bremen, which was a cross-organisational entity set up to develop space technology. This was an amazing feat for such a small German state as the city-state of Bremen.

Manfred Fuchs also got involved in teaching at the University of Applied Sciences, where his former colleague Erich Overesch had since moved. Together, the two friends established a space flight faculty, in which Manfred became honorary professor for "Modern Space Systems", giving him the opportunity to get students interested in space flight and his firm OHB.

Over time, more research facilities and institutes located in Bremen, such as DLR's Institute for Space Flight Systems, the German Research Centre for Artificial Intelligence (DFKI), the Alfred Wegener Institute

for Polar and Marine Research in Bremerhaven and the Institute for Environmental Physics and Remote Sensing. There are now approximately 30 facilities that operate in the field of space flight in the State of Bremen. The small city-state helps to fund this industry and is justified in calling itself a "centre of space flight" by reason of the research activities and two large companies: Airbus Defence and Space (formerly ERNO) and OHB SE. It's not surprising, given the level of competence to be found in Bremen, that major space flight conferences, such as the IAC and COSPAR regularly take place in Bremen.

The drop tower looks down over the Bremen Technology Park from a height of 146 metres and is a symbol of the centre of space flight.

On the bottom is a picture of the inside of the drop tube, in which experiments in free fall are exposed to only one millionth of Earth's gravitational force.

Manfred Fuchs' involvement in the scientific satellite BremSat – shown here with the OHB employee Dieter Wilker – marked his entry into the microsatellite business at the beginning of the 1990s.

SMALL SATELLITES

Electronic components were steadily becoming smaller and smaller, and this brought constant change to satellite development. In the beginning, space flight followed a trend towards ever-larger and more powerful satellites. From as far back as the early days of OHB, Manfred Fuchs had the idea of "bucking the trend and making space flight systems smaller and more affordable". As well as BremSat, OHB got the SAFIR small satellite system off the ground. Smaller satellites cost less to build and had a shorter timeframe for realisation. Therefore more-advanced technologies could be put to use sooner and the launch costs were lower. Plus, in the event of reduced capacities, the gap could be filled in a shorter length of time. From this time on, Manfred Fuchs went by the slogan "small but smart" and – except for the ABRIXAS mission – was very successful with this approach. The contract for the radar reconnaissance satellite SAR-Lupe gave him his break. A string of successes ensued: the Galileo satellites, significant roles in Meteosat Third Generation, EnMAP and SARah. All of the latter are application satellites that are effective and commercial. After populating low-Earth orbit with the smaller OHB satellite systems, Manfred Fuchs put the SmallGEOs on the road to success. These are comparatively small but powerful satellites for geostationary orbit. The first SmallGEO has been in successful operation since the beginning of 2017. Many other models will follow.

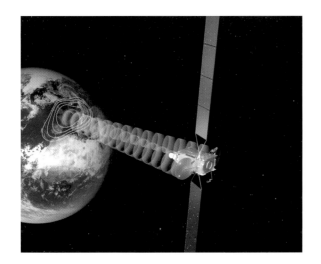

Spaceman extraordinaire Manfred Fuchs gets his break with small satellites. Depicted here are ELECTRA – for use in geostationary orbit – the Earth observation satellite EnMAP, and the separation of the SmallGEO H36W1 from the Soyuz, which has been in successful operation since the end of January 2017.

The MIKROBA parachute to slow down the drop capsule's descent and FALKE models in OHB System's first clean room. Alfred Tegtmeier (left) and Felix Anchuelo discussing the projects.

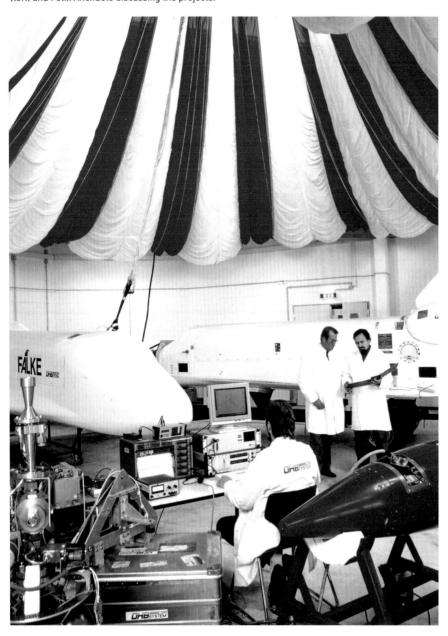

TRANSPORT SYSTEMS

Manfred Fuchs' first taste of space flight was his involvement in the development of the Europa rocket at ERNO. He went on to be instrumental in the development of ARIANE because his Predevelopment department's designs formed the basis for the third stage of the European launch vehicle that is still successful to this day. His specialist subject was propulsion system development because Manfred Fuchs saw launch vehicles as elementary to space flight and ensured that he at least collaborated on the advancement of existing or development of future transport systems. Ultimately, access to space is necessary to exploit space. For that, Europe needed its own launch system to maintain its independence. With that in mind, he also supported the retention of ERNO's test site in Trauen for propulsion unit tests.

Fuchs' range of technological developments for launch systems extends from the failed European bid for a part in the Shuttle project to project roles on Hermes, Phoenix and X-38. Manfred was always at the cutting edge with plans for the latest technological developments, even if these projects got stuck in the blocks for financial reasons. When he went into the satellite business in OHB, he looked around for low-cost launch services for the missions he had planned. He found what he was looking for in Russia. There he reserved a number of low-cost launch slots for the reliable COSMOS launch vehicles. He then worked these into his proposals, giving him a competitive advantage.

In 2005, OHB bought MT Aerospace. In one fell swoop, OHB was the largest German supplier for the ARIANE 5. Commissioned by the ESA, Manfred Fuchs was able to come up with options for the development of new, cheaper and more competitive launch systems thanks to his ideas for effective planning of the new concepts for the ARIANE launch vehicle. Unfortunately, he did not live to see the conclusion of this work. ARIANE 6's maiden launch is scheduled for 2020.

A 1:7 scale model of the Phoenix lander successfully completed its test flight in Sweden in 2004. It was dropped from an altitude of 2,400 metres...

...and, after reaching a top speed of almost 450 km/h in free fall, the prototype landed fully automatically and with pinpoint accuracy in the test airport in Vidsel.

The Moon Village is the vision of ESA Director General
Jan Wörner. He wants to "merge the expertise of various
space-faring nations – be it in the form of robotics or astronauts.
Participants in this permanent Moon base can play a role in a
whole range of fields: science and basic research, commercial
activities, such as extraction of resources, or even tourism."

MOON/MARS

Any spaceman worth his salt dreams of exploring the depths of space. Manfred Fuchs studied in great depth the Big Bang theory and the related questions. Such was his curious mind, he always wanted to go further and further; first to the Moon and then to Mars. He was convinced from a very early stage that these were the next objectives. "Sure, the space station was an incredible achievement, but there was no doubt in our minds that that wasn't the end of manned space flight. It was obvious to people like Manfred Fuchs and Hans Hoffmann that the ISS was just a stepping stone to the Moon and Mars," said Heinz Stoewer.

Manfred's biggest passion was the Moon, the reason being the feasibility of the missions based on existing space technologies, especially existing propulsion units. It would be very difficult, he believed, at least for manned missions, to achieve ranges beyond that. His efforts to convey the benefit of this objective to the people in his circle continued to the end of his days. Even when he was in Predevelopment at ERNO, he had his eye on the Moon and bid for ESA contracts. The exploration of space was already a topic of intense interest for him and he sought out project roles in scientific satellites, such as the astronomy satellite Hipparcos. Of course, his motivations were competitive as well. However, at the back of it all, there was always the desire to participate in the achievement of scientific results through space missions. In his firm, OHB, Manfred Fuchs commissioned studies into how it would be possible to live on the inhospitable surface of the Moon. The question was how to create the environment and the atmosphere in which humans can move about and reside long-term. The matter was given top priority. In addition, he wanted to send his own research satellite to the Moon, Mona Lisa/Moni. Unfor-

tunately, this did not happen in Manfred's lifetime. However, OHB Luxembourg sent the Mission 4M (Manfred Memorial Moon Mission) around the Moon in October 2014 in honour of the founder of the company. The fact that the present ESA Director General Jan Wörner has proposed a Moon Village as space flight's next vision shows that Manfred Fuchs was not wrong on this front either.

Another of Manfred Fuchs' special interests was the exploration and colonisation of the Moon.
Together with his employees, he developed the research station "Mona Lisa" by way of a proposed first step.

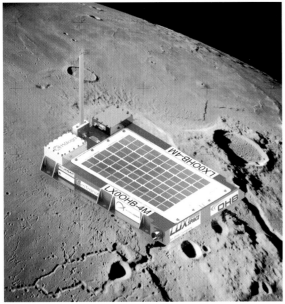

OHB is a major contributor to the satellite for the ExoMars mission. It has been orbiting the Red Planet successfully since 2016.

In honour of Manfred Fuchs, OHB and Luxspace launched the Manfred Memorial Moon Mission on a lunar flyby in October 2014.

SPACE POLITICS

An important factor in the advancement of space flight is political support. Its role was to facilitate the programmes and make the funding available through the agencies in time to carry out the space projects. Spaceman extraordinaire Manfred Fuchs was a pro at using leverage. Early in his career, he assembled a circle of interested parties and supporters around him. As far back as during his time at ERNO he compiled the space programme for the Bremen branch of the CDU. Later, he was responsible for the national CDU space policy in coordination with the South, as a letter of appreciation from Angela Merkel for his work on the election campaign shows. He was also very involved in interest groups that played a supraregional part in what was going on in the world of space flight, such as MESH, DLR, ASU, BDLI, ZARM, CEAS, Eurospace and others, in some of which he was elected to a leadership role. His reputation as a far-sighted, goal-oriented spaceman went so far that he had a leading role in planning the future space flight programme for the ESA.

Former President of the BDLI Hans-Joachim Gante, Federal Minister of the Interior Thomas de Maizière and Manfred Fuchs met at the ILA Berlin Air Show.

Left to right: Volker Kröning (SPD) and Jörg Kastendieck (CDU) accompanied the then Minister for Economics and Technology Michael Glos on a visit to OHB.

Family Fuchs with the Bavarian State Minister of Economic Affairs and Media, Energy and Technology, Ilse Aigner (third from left).

Willi Lemke (left), then mayor of Bremen Jens Böhrnsen (centre) and former CEO of Kaefer Peter Hoedemaker, on a visit to OHB.

Former Ministry Director and Head of the Department of Armaments at the Federal Ministry of Defence Jörg Kaempf is given a model of the SAR-Lupe as a token of appreciation for his visit.

Sharing a joke with Minister of Health Hermann Gröhe and the Bremen CDU's top candidate Elisabeth Motschmann.

Former Federal Minister of the Interior Otto Schily visited the stand at the ILA Berlin Air Show to learn about the SAR-Lupe system.

NETWORK

It is unlikely that Manfred Fuchs would have achieved so much in isolation. His successes and those of the firms ERNO and OHB were due in no small part to the excellent network of experts, policy-makers and friends which Manfred built up and fostered over the course of his life. His standing was based on his expertise but also on his consistency, reliability, fairness and infectious optimism. His great charisma is unforgettable. He used it to create anchor points in business and, above all, in the world of politics, with the aid of movers and shakers; feeding them with information about policy relating to space flight and getting them on board with his visions and projects. Manfred Fuchs was a master at it. He knew which strings to pull to give ideas and projects the momentum to get them realised. He pitched to the agencies; he lobbied to politicians.

When visiting ZARM in Bremen, Mikhail Gorbachev learned a bit about OHB as well; so did former Chancellor Gerhard Schröder at ILA Berlin.

Manfred Fuchs got on well with Evert Dudok (then head of EADS Space) and the agency heads Jan Wörner (formerly of DLR) and Jean-Jacques Dordain (formerly ESA) – also with Airbus chief executive Thomas Enders.

One project that Manfred Fuchs cared deeply about was the Max Valier nano-satellite, which pupils at his alma mater in Bolzano developed and built in conjunction with OHB engineers.

He was also a remarkable judge of human nature. It enabled him to find the right partners for his ideas, visions and projects. Sure, Manfred Fuchs was a strategist. but he was first and foremost genuine. He had a burning passion for space flight and fired up others in his likeable, honest and open way. He was rigorous in maintaining contacts. Many names appear very early on in his records and became permanent fixtures in his professional and private life. However, "you can't rely on being special, you have to be a specialist." This witticism hits the nail on the head, because without his expertise in the field of space flight he would have got no one on side. He was a man of the first hour, had in-depth knowledge and also had very good intuition.

In his lifetime, spaceman extraordinaire Manfred Fuchs was not only involved in space flight and its advancement but also strove to preserve its accomplishments for posterity. His personal work for the German Museum in Munich, where an important space exhibit was curated, is a testament to this. Plus, he later supported the rebuilding of the Johann Hieronymus Schroeter observatory originating from 1782 in Lilienthal near Bremen. However, his real dream was

to open a space museum in his home town of Latsch in South Tyrol. He had found the premises – Annenberg Castle – and had already started on the renovations before he died. Unfortunately, the museum was to be his unfinished opus. Not so the "Max Valier" satellite, however, a project that Manfred Fuchs facilitated for the pupils of his old school in Bolzano, where he began his technical education and which today is called the "Max Valier College of Technology". "It is a first in Europe for schoolgoers to build a satellite – a dream come true," were Manfred Fuchs' own words about this project. So it's fitting that the first radio message sent via the satellite after its launch in June 2017 was "MAX VALIER SAT TNX MANFRED CHRISTA FUCHS".

The globetrotter

A round-the-world trip

"We used to launch rockets in Australia, which is when I discovered Moorea, the most beautiful island in the world," said Manfred Fuchs in an interview with Dolomiten magazine in the year 2000. All his life, the South Tyrolean loved to travel and did so a lot. Following a school trip to Venice and a tour around West Germany during his studies, the aforementioned rocket launches took the curious and cosmopolitan man to Woomera in Australia not long into his career, with a number of stopovers in Asia and French Polynesia along the way. It inspired him to name his later bowling club "Bora Bora". His travel log reveals that he observed everything closely and was fascinated by this "round-the-world trip". Seeing the long queues and two passport control booths in Athens, he suspected that not everyone had the privilege of leaving the country. When they arrived in poverty-stricken Karachi, Pakistan, Manfred was surprised that only a few passengers entered the transit area: "Only five or seven people seemed to want to visit Karachi, even though it has some things worth seeing." He told of his fear of being cheated by money changers and missing out on the cheaper offers. He wrote about crooked taxi drivers whom he eschewed in search of a more honest cabbie. He described the setting: donkey carts, dromedaries and camels carrying loads, craft work on the doorsteps of the houses, dentists plying their trade on the street beside a bowl full of extracted teeth. Manfred speculated, "The larger the bowl, presumably the more experienced the dentist." It is soon evident from the entries that he didn't stay within the confines of the hotels but immersed himself in real life, sought out contact and made observations with curiosity and largely without bias. As it was, his job in space technology involved a lot of business trips – to agencies, project partners, conferences and trade fairs. The nature of the industry is international, so, naturally, Manfred Fuchs travelled all over the world frequently in the course of his life.

In the early years, he took regular trips home to Latsch with Christa, Romana and Marco. Manfred was very attached to South Tyrol and his extended family who lived there. However, as the children got older, it become too monotonous for them and Christa to travel nowhere but back and forth between Bremen and Latsch. They wanted to see more of the world, so alternative holiday destinations were called for. While Latsch was and remained the main destination, the family began to travel more extensively throughout Europe after they had made a stand. Even in his work circles it did not go unnoticed that "Manfred consistently took four or five weeks' holidays with the family every summer," mentioned Gerhard Schneider. He always made time. His family was important to him.

There were also hiking trips with friends in the Alpine Martello Valley in Stelvio Pass National Park, where Manfred Fuchs owned a holiday chalet.

The Fuchs family's wanderlust never abated. The list of countries Manfred and Christa went to together in their lives is long and spans the entire world. Christa was sometimes the one who sought out unusual destinations. "So, of course, I had to go too," Manfred liked to joke. Their packed holiday album contains snaps from destinations such as Yemen, Uzbekistan, Santiago de Compostela, South Africa, Singapore, China as well as the North and South Pole. An exhaustive account of all the places and cultures they visited would fill volumes, so the following pages contain just a selection of glimpses of the Fuchs family's love to travel.

Ladies' Program

Left:
Ladies display the products of their skill at the art of "origami" — paper-folding after a demonstration and lesson at the Takanawatei House in Takanawa Prince Hotel.

Bottom left:
Art enthusiasts try their hand at "sumie" — black ink painting.

Bottom right:
Participants in the visit to a kimono school pose for a picture after serving as models for a demonstration of how to put on and wear kimonos.

Destined for
the top flight

Head in the clouds,
feet on the ground

Flags were important to Manfred Fuchs. For one, to attract attention; for another, to show appreciation to visitors.

From a job with little responsibility to company director and from a small maintenance firm to the top 3 in the European space industry: Manfred Fuchs had a brilliant career, that's plain to see and easy to measure by the results of the space projects he (co-)initiated. In the ERNO days, Manfred Fuchs rose through the ranks relatively quickly – thanks to the success of Spacelab and the later realisation of the European space laboratory Columbus, the establishment of microgravity research, the development of the third stage of the ARIANE rocket and project roles on satellites – to become director of sales for orbital systems, launch systems and drives within twenty years.

After ERNO came OHB, but, though he was its owner and CEO, he had to begin from scratch again. With an initial workforce of five employees and a main line of

work in hydraulics and electronics, OHB was anything but a space company. The rise of OHB is a chapter in the history of an enterprising family, in which Christa, Marco and Manfred Fuchs have all played their part. Manfred's part consisted in driving the development of engineering expertise at OHB. In doing so, he built up its systems capability step by step. He also put an immense amount of energy into kick-starting many projects and steadily expanding the product range. As he did so, he always looked confidently onwards and upwards, and got where he was going, too. He rarely suffered setbacks, but, when he did, as in the case of ABRIXAS or the node for the international space station ISS, he quickly regrouped and generally emerged from the crisis with renewed strength and, in fact, often skipped a couple of rungs on the career ladder in the process.

For Manfred Fuchs, there was no looking back. What was in the past no longer concerned him. After setbacks, in the event of problems or rejections, he used to say, "When the going gets tough, the tough get going." If project partners did not give him his due, he bravely went on the offensive, often at some risk. These actions advanced OHB; for example, SAR-Lupe and Galileo. The two programmes initially seemed beyond OHB's capacity, but Manfred Fuchs wanted a fair share. Both times his competitors denied him that and both

OHB's headquarters (top right; this picture was taken pre-Galileo Integration Hall) is located in Bremen Technology Park.

A picture showing two topics
of importance to Manfred
Fuchs: the Moon and the
visibility of his life's work.

times he had the belief in himself and OHB to bid as main contractor. The outcome is well known and was reported in the media as "David beats Goliath". Manfred Fuchs' meteoric rise to the top was possible because he took well-timed calculated risks.

However, despite being very down to earth, it was important to him to get ahead in his social and personal life. No doubt it's natural for everyone to want that to a certain extent, but it really mattered to Manfred that his success was clearly visible. He got the visibility he craved not by wearing expensive or flashy accessories, but with property. When he moved his as-yet small firm into the new premises on Universitätsallee in October 1988, the first item on the hand-written agenda was the topic of flags. He wanted flags to signal to the world: here is someone of importance and that someone is OHB! Ever since then, the company and national flag have flown proudly in front of all of OHB's office buildings. Foreign visitors are sometimes greeted with their national flags as a token of appreciation.

He also used signage to raise OHB's profile. For example, Fuchs Gruppe is spelt out in large letters beside the name OHB on top of the company headquarters in Bremen Technology Park.

Getting exposure for himself and his family's name was important to him. He wanted to exhibit his achievements and receive recognition for them. For example, after the engineering school he had attended in Hamburg was renamed Hamburg University of Applied Sciences, he had his diploma officially reissued and hung up in his office. He also used his honorary titles "professor" and "Dr h.c." with pride. Even his wife often called him "professore" in allusion to his Italian roots. He had the many awards and honours he received

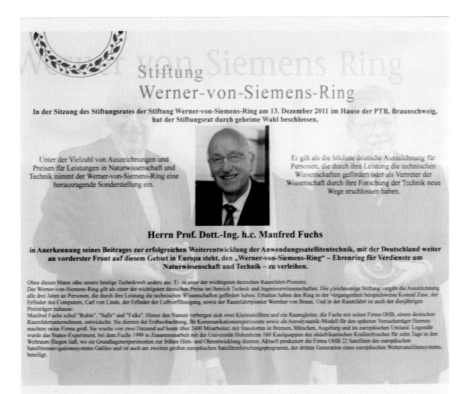

nicely framed and prominently displayed them in the management quarters of OHB.

Manfred Fuchs' motivation to seek out prestige presumably stems from his circumstances growing up in South Tyrol. His father Romedius' success in business was not as brilliant as that of his siblings. "He may have had a small haulage business but then there were the 'big shots' who had a sawmill and the like – their success was more visible," said Marco Fuchs, who suspects this may be the reason for his father's latent ambition to be a success for the sake of the family honour.

The Werner von Siemens Ring was one of the highest honours bestowed upon Manfred Fuchs.

Though Manfred Fuchs (second from left in this picture taken at the school championships) was not particularly sporty, he had the Olympic spirit in him from an early age: citius, altius, fortius – faster, higher, stronger.

"Space flight was something completely new and held the prospect of making it to the very top."

In fact, Manfred Fuchs' upward mobility is a classic example of the American Dream.

He arrived in Germany from South Tyrol with nothing but a suitcase. All his belongings were contained in that one case, which is still kept in the attic of his house in Huchting. Through determination, modesty and hard work during his studies, he climbed the career ladder rung by rung. The first member of the Fuchs clan to go to college, he started out at Hamburger Flugzeugbau (HFB) and thus began his social ascent.

The rented student room gave way to a large apartment in a grand Hamburg villa. When the opportunity came his way to move to the newly established Entwicklungsring Nord in Bremen, he seized it. Of his motivation, his wife Christa said, "Things at HFB were fine and interesting enough, but most of the posts, especially those higher up, were already taken. Space flight was something completely new and held the prospect of making it to the very top."

This account also corroborates his friend Sepp Rinner's description of Manfred as a "sly dog". It suggests that one of the reasons why he chose Bremen was "because he undoubtedly knew that he would have an easier 'in' to the small community and political life. Social and political access would have been more difficult and protracted in Munich or Hamburg."

Two Galileo satellites being prepared for their launch aboard the Soyuz in Kourou, French Guiana.

House and Opel Adimral; one of the popular basement parties at the Fuchs' family home.

When it became clear in 1964 that the Fuchs family was moving to Bremen, Manfred Fuchs hastily bought a terraced house in Bremen-Huchting. According to Marco, it was normal for Manfred to make this kind of financial commitment. Anyone else would have waited to see how the job went, but Manfred invested immediately in a property near his place of work. The family thought he was crazy. As it happened, they didn't set eyes on the house until the day of the move. However, he did say straight off that it was only a temporary solution, that he planned to buy a larger, detached house in the foreseeable future.

In Huchting, the family initially lived a very normal middle-class life for the burgeoning German economy. The residents of these newly constructed terraced houses had a similar social background. The men had good jobs, the women stayed at home and cared for the children. They took holidays and threw parties in their basement bars. Romana and Marco went to the local grammar school and earned some extra pocket money by gathering up shopping trolleys in the Roland-Center mall, around which life for the Huchting locals revolved. "Everything was pretty stereotypical," said Marco in summary. As was the fact that as the children got older his mother began to feel couped up and got herself a part-time job. What was unusual for the time was that Romana and Marco were sent to one of the few all-day schools in the area because their mother did not like cooking. "We did not get home until 4 pm because we ate lunch at school. In the 1970s that was very unusual," recalled Romana.

"He was not afraid of losing social status, nor did he have to try too hard to maintain his position."

As promised, after ten or so very happy years in the terraced house, the family moved to a more prestigious property in an estate of detached houses in Bremen-Huchting. Again, "from the outset the plan was to alter and extend the property," remarked Christa. Even before they moved in, they knocked out a wall between the living room and the kitchen, made the cooking area smaller and built a conservatory off the living area. They had a wooden cabin built in the garden, which reminded Manfred of his native South Tyrol. He liked to retire here when the sun shone and enjoyed the aroma of timber as he pored over his newspapers. At that time, he was still working high up at ERNO and the children were still dependent on him. However, after he became a successful entrepreneur with OHB, the house underwent further remodelling. During a tour of the southern states of America, Manfred Fuchs admired the imposing houses reminiscent of "Gone with the Wind". It seems he was so taken with them that he wanted a similar mansion himself. Back in Bremen, he commissioned his architects to add another wing, a central entrance and a portico to the front. Such was

The cabin in the garden was a reminder of his native South Tyrol and a bolthole for reading the paper.

After it was renovated, the house in Huchting looked like something from "Gone with the Wind", so friends of the Fuchs family dressed up in southern costumes.

the similarity to Tara, the O'Hara plantation house, that, as a joke, the family's Bremen friends dressed up as southern belles and beaus for a party at the Fuchs'.

In his native South Tyrol, too, Manfred Fuchs "collected" apartments, houses and holdings, culminating in an imposing castle. This satisfied his need for visibility and for keeping up the family honour and, at the same time, gave something back to his native community. He was a poster child for the South Tyrolean self-made man, a welcome interviewee and in 2008 was listed among the 50 richest South Tyrolean by the weekly magazine ff.

Despite all the possessions Manfred Fuchs had and could have had, he remained down to earth at all times. With the exception of his generosity, his wealth did not affect his personality. His success never went to his head: on the contrary, he was conscious of his roots. According to Marco Fuchs, his father "was not afraid of losing social status, nor did he have to try too hard to maintain his position." His standing was more or less a natural consequence of his having the right professional and personal skills.

While his professional and private successes pleased him, Manfred Fuchs wanted to press onwards and upwards. He never had any doubt about making it. Manfred was a very self-confident and, above all, optimistic man with a clear vision. This also extended to his involvement in politics. He could easily have achieved more for himself within the CDU party. When Bernd Neumann was in office, he offered Manfred the position of Senator for Economic Affairs. No doubt it was tempting for Manfred Fuchs, go-getter that he was, but he did not stray from the course he had plotted for himself. He mentioned it in his diary in July 2004: "Turned down the offer to become Senator for Economic

A humorous host, Manfred Fuchs even stood on chairs to give his speeches.

Manfred Fuchs and Bernd Neumann at the official opening of the Columbus Integration Hall. The entrepreneur did not pursue a political career – to the benefit of his firm OHB.

Affairs... I can't leave the firm just yet... If I left OHB now, Bremen would probably lose more than it gained!" The reason Manfred Fuchs gave for his decision was the upcoming negotiations on company takeovers and the company's biggest proposal to date, which was being prepared at that time. Romana saw her father's involvement in politics as very pragmatic: "He was in

politics for the sake of space flight. His primary interest was the space industry. For him, politics was a means by which to do something positive for space flight. He was on the Parliament of Bremen committee but never harboured any ambitions to become mayor or governor of Bremen." According to his son, Manfred Fuchs had always been that bit more ambitious and gave his children the impression that they were "better off". Not better than other people or of a higher social class but materially better off. Manfred Fuchs was actually a real people person. He had a genuine interest in others, no matter where they came from or what their position was. He was able to chat just as easily with the cleaning staff of his firm as with the "boys" on the executive floor. He never forgot his roots, remained true to himself and was always authentic.

His used his positive attitude and charm to build up his network and to bring his plans to fruition. His healthy measure of self-confidence, his assertiveness and his in-depth knowledge of space flight got him far. All of that made him a go-getter in a positive sense, not a careerist concerned only with his own personal advancement. He wasted no time – in fact, it was back in the ERNO days – in securing a place in the right space circles to give him a key role in the advancement of European space flight in the agencies ESA and DLR and the industrial associations, such as the M.E.S.H. consortium, the SME Space Alliance and the BDLI. In one of his final roles, as coordinator for the space industry for 2013/2014, appointed by the then Director General of the ESA, Jean-Jacques Dordain, he helped to write the ESA's agenda for the coming years.

ESA directors visiting OHB in Bremen: Alain Bories, Karlheinz Kreuzberg, Fritz Merkle, Dieter Birreck, Magali Vaissiere, Giuseppe Morsillo, Ingo Engeln, Manfred Fuchs, Jean-Jacques Dordain, Franco Ongaro, Jochen Schaper, Didier Faivre, Hans J. Steininger, Volker Liebig, Roberto Aceti, Thomas Reiter, Gierth Olsson, Wolfgang Konrad, Frank Negretti and Markus Katzkowski.

Thanks to his employees, Manfred Fuchs owned a piece of land on the Moon, an object of fascination for him all his life.

ZERTIFIKAT

über ein Grundstück auf dem Erdenmond
von der Fläche 1.000 m².

Es befindet sich auf der uns zugewandten Seite des Mondes
in der Gegend um 58° nördliche Breite und 54° östliche Länge.

Area	Quadrant	Lot	Land
B-12	Bravo	64	mo-e-3241

Eingetragener Eigentümer ist:

Manfred Fuchs

Die Registrierung erfolgt mit sofortiger Wirkung im Mondregister
der Firma ASTROX, welche dieses Mondgrundstück offiziell von
der Lunar Embassy in den USA erworben hat.
Beurkundet am 18. Juli 2008.

Holger Czajka,
Geschäftsführer Firma ASTROX

From "Medl Fuchs' young lad" to the head of a space empire with 2,400 employees, Manfred Fuchs climbed to incredible heights, both professionally and privately. The Pope congratulated him and his wife on their golden wedding anniversary and Chancellor Merkel thanked him personally for his services. However, Manfred Fuchs was just as pleased with the imaginative birthday presents he received from his staff: a piece of land on the Moon and a telescope, with which he liked to gaze at the stars, to which he, or so he himself believed, ascended on 26th April 2014.

Quotes

"Manfred Fuchs is someone who turns on the light rather than grumble about the dark; someone who believes the only wrong is losing one's nerve."

Dr Christine Backhaus, Bremer Unternehmer, 2nd quarter 1996

"OHB is always a reliable, trusted partner and a source of inspiration and visionary strength."

Prof. Dr Hansjörg Dittus, Chairman of the Executive Board at DLR,
at the official opening of the Galileo Hall in June 2012, Wirtschaft in Bremen

"Spiritual father of space flight."

W&W Bremen's family business magazine, Volker Schwennen, Jan–Mar 2013

"OHB AG is a poster child for Germany as a high-tech business location. It is an SME with a hugely successful blend of vision and cutting-edge technology."

Philipp Rösler, Wirtschaft in Bremen, 06/11

"Modern space flight would not be what it is today without Manfred Fuchs."

Südtirol Panorama, Melanie Ockert, June 2009

"I was born optimistic."

Manfred Fuchs

"Manfred Fuchs was a business celebrity in Bremen."

Christoph Weiss, President of the Bremen Chamber of Commerce obituary June 2014

"The light of those who shine bright will shine long."

Uwe Schmaling, Raumfahrt Concret obituary 3.14

"Manfred Fuchs and his company shaped space flight in Europe."

Weser-Kurier obituary, Maren Benecke, 29th April 2014

"I hit upon the idea of bucking the trend and making space flight systems smaller and more affordable."

Manfred Fuchs

"With Manfred Fuchs gone, Bremen has lost a pioneer of the aerospace industry and an entrepreneur in the truest sense of the word."

Former mayor Jens Böhrnsen and Senator for Economic Affairs Martin Günthner,

Senate press releases, 28th April 2014

"With the passing of Professor Manfred Fuchs, the Bremen CDU has lost a prominent personality, a major supporter and a loyal friend and advisor. He had a visionary influence on Bremen as a centre of technology and his lifetime of enterprise has helped Bremen to become a global technology leader in today's space industry."

Jörg Kastendiek, leader of CDU Bremen, BundesPressePortal, 28th April 2014

"In a time when political direction was lacking and the space industry was dominated by conglomerates and state consortia, Fuchs steered his SME to immense success through innovation, willingness to take risks and determination."

Stefan Thews, regional chairman of the BJU, address at Bremen Entrepreneur of the Year ceremony 1996

"There are career men. There are career women. There are career couples, each with their own career. And then there's the husband and wife team of Christa and Manfred Fuchs."

Dr Christine Backhaus, Bremer Unternehmer, 2nd quarter 1996

Impressions

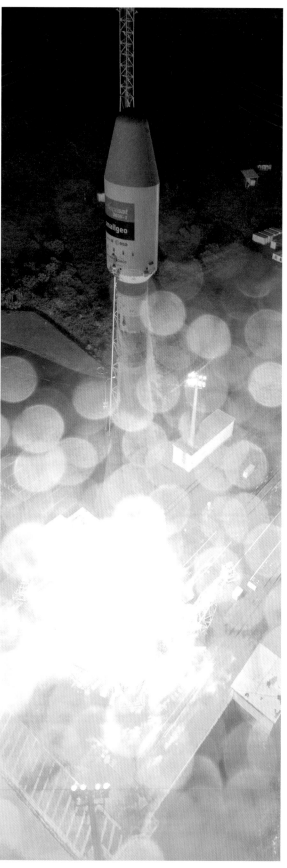

Epilogue

Epilogue

How do you create a new way of thinking? What makes people get behind a bold idea? And just how much courage and willingness to take risks are required to turn a vision into reality? These questions are very closely linked to terms such as disruption, digitisation and start-ups. However, the discussion which has been ongoing for some time in connection with these terms gives the wrong impression as to how, for many generations now, technological and, in turn, economic progress have been achieved. Disruption is not a new phenomenon. In the past, however, it was referred to more prosaically as the innovation process. Start-ups are also nothing new, yet previously they bore the somewhat less spectacular name of new companies.

Back then, the individuals behind these enterprises were driven by the same motivation as young and dynamic digital natives in the start-up scene today. They, too, were in search of the "next big thing", that one innovation which would turn their company into something special, the innovation which would result in the next major technological advance.

Over 30 years ago, OHB was a start-up before the term had even been invented. OHB is the classic story of a company which started in a garage and went on to become a major enterprise.

The driving force and ingenious visionary behind this story was my father, Manfred Fuchs. He set his sights on the niche of smaller, lighter and thus cheaper satellites during a time when only very people understood the economical advantages this could unleash. Given the knowledge we have today, this development barely seems impressive, yet the decisions he took back then were nothing short of spectacularly brave. And that is precisely what makes his achievements truly exceptional, and why we are so full of admiration for him. He possessed the ability to understand and indeed have a vision of where developments would lead. Or, as put so aptly by the Anglo-Irish author Jonathan Swift: "Vision is the art of seeing what is invisible to others." Yet to be a successful entrepreneur, you need more than just this. Being an ingenious visionary is very handy when you need exceptional ideas. However, in order to turn these ideas into reality, you also need courage and self-confidence. My father was also not short on these qualities.

More than 30 years ago, the projects which he was driving forwards seemed, at best, bold and, at worst, insane. What's more, the "professor", as my mother often referred to him, was more than happy to refer to himself as crazy! And whenever a member of staff approached him with a bold suggestion, he would laugh heartily, saying: "We have another crazy guy here! Brilliant! These are precisely the people we need to stay in the game."

The foundation which he laid at OHB is based on the unshakeable belief in the strength of his vision, in the constructive effects of enabling free thought and the continuous pursuit of ever better, more exceptional ideas. He always wanted to go where there were new things to be discovered, and was interested in issues in their entirety. I have to admit that I have a great deal of respect for the optimism which he exuded and, above all, for his ability to infect others with this enthusiasm thanks to his empathetic nature. My father's optimism has also been a major source of courage for me in light of the many tasks which the company faces. It's difficult to put into words, but I believe that this courage can be simply put down to the basic sense of trust which children have in their parents. This also goes some way to explaining the secret of the success of German family companies: If my father took on projects with childlike curiosity, courage and optimism, then there must be something fundamentally right about this approach.

Indeed, this methodology has proven successful time and time again in numerous projects. Even today, it still fills me with enthusiasm when I recall the passion, pioneering spirit, geniality and cross-cultural warmth my father displayed when working together with the Russians. Courage was required again there, as the Iron Curtain had only recently fallen. Yet, at the same time, this courage came with the promise of business success. And, for the most part, this resulted in impressive successes.

In many ways he was ahead of his time in the search for new, ever better ideas. He always dreamed of a "Bremen Silicon Valley", where free spirits would be able to let their imaginations run wild in search of the "next big thing". It's no coincidence that 30 years ago he commissioned a garden and pond for the first building we owned in the Universitätsallee. For him it was important that employees at OHB had the space to think.

Today, his spirit and approach are more tangible than ever before in the company. The future of OHB also lies in new space: in that area of modern space travel which requires huge amounts of creativity to transform space technology into earthly business models. However, my father's fundamental mission still applies today. It states: at OHB, we make space travel simpler, more efficient and therefore more cost-effective. In today's new space market, this mission statement has been expanded to include the promise of committing to the development of solutions which will be beneficial to humankind, society and tomorrow's world.

It will only be possible to follow through on this promise if we embrace Manfred Fuchs' spirit in moving forward. Above all, this means fostering and developing his enthusiasm for visionaries, his absolute desire to discover new approaches, his almost childlike love of technology and space travel in all areas of the company. OHB was a start-up when the word didn't even exist. Looking ahead, despite being an established company in the space travel market, OHB needs to recapture the mentality of a start-up.

Space travel is starting to dream big again, and we can use these opportunities for extraordinary projects and missions. OHB was and remains open to missions with the potential to expand the boundaries of what we know and what has been conceivable to date. For example, the so-called "chipsats" from the Breakthrough initiative are travelling on the Max Valier satellite. A fascinating idea of reaching the nearest solar system, Alpha Centauri, with very many so-called Femto satellites (with a maximum mass in the double-digit gram range). My father would have loved this mission. And I am sure he would have stopped at nothing to be involved. Perhaps that is why I didn't hesitate for a second when OHB was presented with the opportunity to participate. One of the enduring goals for a space company must be involvement in fascinating missions, and that means I sometimes have to put economic interests to one side, if only briefly. In addition to projects which serve the necessary corporate goals, a number of projects of a visionary scientific nature must also be pursued. That is not just important for society, but also for the company: staff at OHB should come to work every day with the sense of being involved in something special.

As fascinating as this journey to the nearest star, some 4.4 light years or 41 billion kilometres away, may appear, it will be almost impossible to cover this distance in a lifetime. That's why, activities focusing on the Moon have become increasingly appealing. Relatively speaking, the Earth's moon is just round the corner. There has been no human on the Moon's surface since 1972. Over the past 45 years, we have seen enormous technological advances in all areas of humanity. It would be truly exciting to discover how these developments could be used today on the Moon. It is a well-known fact that my father was always extremely enthusiastic about the idea of a new Moon mission. Indeed, ten years ago, this almost became a reality at national level. OHB, for one, would be extremely keen to get involved in a mission of this kind, not least as this would allow one of my father's greatest legacies to be realised. The 4M mission to the Moon shortly following his death was a spontaneous tribute to this. A German or European mission to the Moon would be the perfect project to honour the visionary spirit, overwhelming optimism and curiosity of Manfred Fuchs.

On behalf of the Board, the Supervisory Board and the entire team at OHB, I sincerely hope that you enjoy reading this book!

We would like to express our gratitude to the two authors, Danela Sell and Joachim Thaeter, for this truly great book and for all the hard work involved in realising this project. I am certain that my father would have loved it.

Yours,

Marco R. Fuchs

The Board which will guide
OHB in the future (from left):
Klaus Hofmann,
Marco R. Fuchs and
Dr Fritz Merkle.

Prof. Heinz Stoewer,
Christa Fuchs and
Robert Wethmar, LL.M
make up the Supervisory
Board at OHB SE.

Photo credits

ACKNOWLEDGEMENTS

We wish to thank all those we interviewed and everyone who made this book possible by sharing their experiences with us and giving us an insight into the eventful life of Manfred Fuchs.

We thank his family in particular for speaking so openly about the private side of their husband, brother, father, grandfather and father-in-law.

Our sincere thanks go to Bernd Neumann, Prof. Ernesto Vallerani and Prof. Heinz Stoewer for the forewords to this book and the valuable interviews.

We greatly appreciate the assistance, especially of Dr Edith Götsch, Romed and Günther Fuchs, with our research in South Tyrol. They provided us with information and some historical images when we couldn't be there ourselves.

It would not have been possible to produce the book in this quality without the hard work of layout artist Sara Lünemann, the proofreaders at Textgärtnerei – Bernd Degener, Kristina Kreitz und Martin Radke – and the print specialists at Berlin Druck.

For the English translation, which captured the style of the original, we would like to thank Michelle Austin and proofreaders Fiona Moore and Michael Wright at Synonym Translations.

Special thanks also go to our publisher Carl Ed. Schünemann. We could not have wished for a more fitting distribution partner than a Bremen family business steeped in tradition.

Many thanks also go to all the employees of the OHB Group, to all the friends and the private, professional and political associates of Manfred Fuchs, to the many journalists whose articles and interviews have preserved history and contributed to this book either directly or indirectly.

Last but not least, we extend a big Thank You to Manfred Fuchs himself, who, it is plain to see, enriched the lives of so many people in his inimitable way, with his empathy and his undiminished optimism. Many families across Europe today owe their livelihood to his willingness to take risks and his success in business.

Below is a list of the people (in alphabetical order) whom we would like to thank for the interviews, the images, the documents and their assistance both at OHB and in South Tyrol:

A

Michelle Austin

B

Dr Christine Backhaus
Michael Bahlo
Carsten Baucke
Maren Benecke
Jens Böhrnsen
Alain Bories
Ulrich Bremer

D

Bernd Degener
Prof. Dr Hansjörg Dittus

O

Melanie Ockert
Gierth Olsson
Nurlan Onzhanov
Enrique Ortiz Walter
Prof. Erich Overesch (†)
Janne Overesch

P

Alain Pajonk

R

Martin Radke
Prof. Hans Rath (†)
Sabine von der Recke
Julia Riedl
Erika Rinner
Josef (Sepp) Rinner
Alexander Rolfsen

S

Henning Scherf
Uwe Schmaling
Martin Scherenberger
Gerhard Schneider
Dr Rüdiger Schönfeld
Günther Schöpf
Hermann Schünemann
Ulrich Schulz
Veronika Sell
Hans J. Steininger
Reinhard Stelljes
Prof. Heinz Stoewer
Aloisia (Luise) Stricker

T

Stefan Thews
Prof. Dr Helmuth Trischler

V

Paul Vahlenkamp
Angelo Vallerani
Prof. Ernesto Vallerani

W

Ingo Wagner
Petra Wiertellorz
Christoph Weiss
Dr Barbara Willimek
Arne Winterboer
Johann-Dietrich "Jan" Wörner
Marianne Wosala
Michael Wright

Imprint

The German National Library has registered this publication in the German National Bibliography: detailed bibliographical data can be found online at http://dnb.dnb.de.

Carl Schünemann Verlag GmbH, Bremen, Germany
www.schuenemann-verlag.de

© 2018 OHB SE
Karl-Ferdinand-Braun-Str.8
28359 Bremen

1st edition 2018

Authors/text: Danela Sell & Joachim Thaeter

Book design and typesetting: Sara Lünemann

Translation: Michelle Austin

German proofreading: Textgärtnerei, Bremen

English proofreading: Synonym Translations, Bremen

Print: BerlinDruck

Printed in Germany

ISBN 978-3-96047-038-7